CONVERTS TO JUDAISM

CONVERTS TO JUDAISM

Stories from Biblical Times to Today

Lawrence J. Epstein

ROWMAN & LITTLEFIELD
Lanham • Boulder • New York • London

Published by Rowman & Littlefield
A wholly owned subsidiary of
The Rowman & Littlefield Publishing Group, Inc.
4501 Forbes Boulevard, Suite 200, Lanham, Maryland 20706
www.rowman.com

Unit A, Whitacre Mews, 26-34 Stannary Street, London SE11 4AB,
United Kingdom

British Library Cataloguing in Publication Information Available

Library of Congress Cataloging-in-Publication Data
Epstein, Lawrence J. (Lawrence Jeffrey)
Converts to Judaism : stories from biblical times to today / Lawrence J. Epstein.
pages cm
Includes bibliographical references and index.
ISBN 978-1-4422-3467-3 (cloth : alk. paper) — ISBN 978-1-4422-3468-0
(electronic)
1. Conversion—Judaism—History. 2. Jewish converts—Biography. I. Title.
BM729.P7E664 2015
296.7'10922—dc23
2014034409

Printed in the United States of America

This book is dedicated to my grandchildren
Lily, Grayson, and Emilia Rose

CONTENTS

PREFACE

In about 1140, the Spanish Jewish philosopher Yehuda Halevi wrote a book widely known as the *Kuzari*. The book is a dialogue between the king of a group of people called the Khazars and a rabbi. The king is trying to figure out which religion his people should follow. As Halevi constructs the debate, the rabbi does not offer logical proofs of God's existence. Instead, the rabbi considers Jewish history as a key to understanding the Jewish people. The rabbi recounts how Jews were able to survive after losing their nation and so consistently facing poverty and persecution. How, he wonders, could they maintain their faith and their reliable moral compass in the most hostile conditions life offers?

Prompted by Halevi's approach, I want in this book to examine an underappreciated part of that history, the contributions converts to Judaism have made to the Jewish people and the Jewish religion. The book isn't an argument to welcome converts, although in the last chapter I will provide the sort of argument that is inherent in Jewish history. Instead, I provide this history because I believe it offers the best proof that encouraging converts to Judaism is codified in Jewish law, coheres with the most basic beliefs of Judaism, is part of the Jewish spiritual vocation, has a noble past filled with colorful characters, and offers a promising future. I am not unaware of or indifferent to the communal concerns some people have about conversions. I try in this volume to discuss every one of those concerns in a fair way.

History is vital to the Jewish people. Jews believe in their shared destiny, in the significance of their historic spiritual journey, and so in the significance of every act they undertake, seeing it as accelerating or retarding their personal spiritual growth and the achievement of a better world. Jews see themselves as partners with God in the ongoing work of creation, and so every person and every contribution is vital, every day a chance for renewal, every adversity a hurdle to be leaped. In this book, I try to show that converts have contributed immensely as the Jewish people traversed paths through a sometimes painfully difficult world. The book traces the history of conversion to Judaism in Jewish life, the legal tangles, the attractions of the Jewish faith, the resistance to converts that grew, and the fate of conversion in the story of the Jewish people.

I've had a long-standing interest in the subject of converts to Judaism. Many people assume that there must be a personal reason for this interest. There is a reason, but it is not obvious. My wife, for example, was born Jewish. I don't know of any of my or her ancestors who were converts. Indeed, I am a Kohen, a purported descendant of Aaron and therefore from a priestly class not allowed to marry converts in traditional Judaism. My interest is therefore not familial, but it is autobiographical. While I was born and raised as a Jew, I had no emotional connection to being Jewish, no strong ties. And then, in my early twenties, I went on a search for faith, much like the king of the Khazars, but, unlike the king, I found that faith in my own spiritual backyard. My "conversion" to Judaism wasn't literal, but I intensely identified with all those people who, having sought and searched, found in Judaism the guidelines for believing and living.

I began to study why converts joined the Jewish people. I wrote some books about conversion, including a guidebook for those who wished to become Jewish. As I talked to many people, I realized that converts were not always understood, that all they had given to their adopted people were too often hidden gifts.

This book is an attempt to give converts their true and justified place in Jewish history.

I start with an overview of the subject and then proceed era by historical era, starting naturally with biblical times. As I proceed, the converts discussed are put in historical context. It is crucial to understand, for example, the immense spiritual and often physical courage that converts had to face and the arc of Jewish efforts to encourage their conversion and welcome them to Jewish life. This courage often included confronting the persecution they faced for joining the Jewish people. The story of welcoming converts also includes withdrawing from such activities on a widespread basis and, slowly, recovering the initial impulse to welcome new Jews. I also try to trace the evolution of conversion in Jewish law to see how it adapted and found a place for converts. I offer an interpretation that encouraging converts is a mandated task for the Jewish people, that Jews should welcome sincere converts without using any pressure on them. This interpretation is embedded in the historical march of the book.

All writers are reluctant to fence off the intended readership of their books, to limit those who might find it useful. But I did have certain audiences in mind as I planned this work. I hope, in particular, that converts, would-be converts, their friends, and their families will find support in these pages as they witness the unfolding pageant of the people they or their loved ones join. I wanted to write for Jews who remain suspicious of converts, who wonder whether they are genuinely Jewish or what they can add to Jewish life. The book is meant for anyone interested in religious history, Jewish history, and the individual soul's sometimes disquieting, often heroic, struggle to find a home.

I invite you, the reader, also to explore the mysteries of the past, to see the staggering ways history has shaped all of us. History is within us, and we are within history. Knowing our past, carrying it with us, helps us understand who we are, how we got here, and where we might go. Jewish history is surely unique. The Jews have been everywhere, encountered every hostility the cosmos can throw at a people, and endured seemingly unendurable suffering, yet here we are, still struggling, still fueled by a fire in every vein, still curious about tomorrow. The Jewish story is a good one to follow, and the place of converts in that story has within it more than a few surprises.

ACKNOWLEDGMENTS

The subject of conversion to Judaism has interested me for a long while, and my debt to all those who have studied and written about the subject, who have talked to me about it, who have undertaken the journey to Judaism themselves, and who have provided advice and materials is enormous. I could start with the people throughout Jewish history who have been interested in this subject and, through their efforts, fascinated me.

More exactly, I could go back to each of the articles and books I wrote about conversion and thank everyone who helped with those. My writing books about conversion began with Arthur Kurzweil, then at Jason Aronson Inc., who, knowing of my interest in the subject, suggested I write a guidebook for converts. I interviewed hundreds of converts and many experts for that book. I corresponded or spoke profitably with a variety of people. They included Rabbi Marc Angel, Prof. Nicholas de Lange, Leonard Fein, Dr. Louis Feldman, Rabbi Steven E. Foster, Dr. Robert Gordis, of blessed memory, Julius Lester, Dennis Prager, and many others. They provided some of the foundation for my thinking.

The literature on conversion to Judaism is nowhere conveniently collected, yet there is a lot of it. To get at it required a sustained effort by archivists and librarians to help me locate some of the material. I've worked with people at literally dozens of libraries. I thank the American Jewish Historical Society, the Jewish Theological Seminary of America Library, the Asher Library of the Spertus College of Judaica, the *Jerusalem Post* archives, the Jewish Division of the New York Public Library, the Hebrew University of Jerusalem, the Hebrew Union College Jewish Institute of Religion Library, the Harvard University Library, and so many others. I want to thank particularly Kevin Proffitt of the American Jewish Archives. I have called on him many times to get material, and he has always provided what I needed in a timely and useful fashion.

There are some people mentioned in this book who were crucial in the history of conversion to Judaism who helped me along the way. They include Rabbi Moshe M. Maggal, who invited me to serve as vice president of the National Jewish Information Service, David Horowitz, and Rabbi Alexander Schindler, who gave me an extraordinarily extensive interview about his famous conversion proposal. It was this interview that became the basis for my first article about conversion.

For this particular book, I got advice from numerous people.

They include Rabbi Stephen Karol, Rabbi Adam Fisher, Dr. Harry Ostrer, Rabbi Dana Evan Kaplan, Rabbi Haim Beliak, Rabbi Leah Cohen, Dr. Lawrence Grossman, Dr. Seth Forman, Dawn Kepler, Sue Fishkoff, Nan Gefen, Rabbi Adam Greenwald, Rabbi David J. B. Krishef, Rabbi Elliot Cosgrove, Rabbi Carol Levithan, Rabbi Steve Fox, Rabbi Jonathan Lubliner, Rabbi Sharon Brous, Rabbi Laura Geller, and Rabbi Ed Feinstein. I also got advice from several people who deserve historical credit for writing about conversion for a very long time. They include Rabbi Steven Foster, Rabbi Allen Maller, and Rabbi Gilbert Kollin. In fact, it was an article I read by Rabbi Kollin early in 1975 that first introduced me to the subject of conversion to Judaism.

There is a reason authors are so careful to point out that any mistakes in the book are the authors' alone and are not due to the people who helped them. That is certainly true in this book, and if I have made errors in fact or interpretation, I bear responsibility for them despite the best efforts of all these people to lead me to the truth.

I would also like to thank Sarah Stanton and the entire professional and dedicated staff at Rowman & Littlefield as well as an anonymous academic reviewer of the book who read the manuscript with enormous care and provided valuable material.

Of course, it is impossible to write any book without the constant support of a family. In this regard, I have been particularly fortunate. My parents, Fred and Lillian Epstein, of blessed memory, always encouraged my writing efforts. My brother, Richard, is my first reader for all my books. He has listened patiently across the years to many discussions about conversion. His wife, Perla, and their children, Adam and Sondra and their families, are always supportive.

My children and their spouses, Michael Epstein and Sophia Cacciola, Elana and Justin Reiser, Rachel and John Eddey, and Lisa and Florian Christen are all great, warm, kind, and supportive people.

My grandchildren, in birth order, are Lily Reiser, Grayson Eddey, and Emilia Rose Christen. The book's dedication to them is a small indication of the comfort they bring to me, the promise of a great future that they offer.

Finally, my wife, Sharon, is there every hour of every day to provide love and companionship, support and advice. The importance of her presence in my life is immeasurable.

INTRODUCTION: WELCOMING THE STRANGER

The Place of Converts in Jewish Life

He was the first US consul to Jerusalem, originally drawn to the sacred land to become a missionary to the Jewish people. But, as it does to so many people, Jerusalem had a dazzling effect on him. He came more and more to identify with the Jewish people, and eventually, against the advice of the local rabbi, he converted to Judaism. When he returned to his home in Philadelphia, his wife and family, shocked at his religious conclusions, had him put in a mental hospital. A court ruled him insane.

His name was Warder Cresson, and the appeal of his conviction at a lunacy trial in 1851 attracted national attention and fervent discussion. The trial raised crucial questions about religious freedom in the United States and about what it meant for a Gentile to become Jewish. Eventually, the jury declared Cresson innocent. It was judged not a sign of insanity to become Jewish.

Cresson then returned to the Holy Land. There he met Herman Melville and John Steinbeck's grandfather, among others. Cresson became the model of a character in Melville's book-length poem *Clarel*. Once back in the land he felt to be his spiritual home, Cresson tried to teach farming to the Jewish community, remarried, and had two children. He died in 1860. All Jewish-owned businesses in Jerusalem were closed on the day of his funeral.

Having to endure an accusation of insanity was not the worst fate a convert to Judaism has suffered in Jewish history. Count Valentine Potocki was a Polish nobleman. According to Jewish sources, Potocki and a friend were in Paris studying when they entered a wine shop and became interested in the owner, who was studying the Talmud. The two friends asked the old man questions about the Hebrew Bible, and, entranced, they requested that he teach them Hebrew. They vowed to become Jews themselves if they could be convinced of Judaism's truth. After six months of study, the friends realized how attracted they were to Judaism. At that time, the first half of the eighteenth century, Amsterdam was the rare European place where a Gentile could embrace Judaism. Potocki went to Amsterdam, became Jewish, and took the name Abraham ben Abraham. He returned to Poland but sought to remain anonymous because there in his home country it was illegal, under penalty of death, to abandon Christianity for Judaism. Potocki was eventually betrayed and arrested. The authorities and his family begged him to renounce Judaism, but Potocki would not do so. He suffered a long imprisonment until he was burned at the stake on May 24, 1749. Tragically, the king had written a letter of pardon for Potocki, but it arrived too late to save him. A supporter bribed a guard to secure his ashes, and those ashes of a Jewish martyr were later buried in the Jewish cemetery. Eventually a tree grew over the burial place and became a destination for pilgrimages by Jews. Vandals ultimately desecrated the gravesite.

Of course, most conversion stories end more happily. There are, though, a lot of unusual conversion stories. One of the strangest involves Reuel Abraham. His birth name was Karl Heinz Schneider. He spent his teen years organizing Nazi youth battalions. At age eighteen, he volunteered for combat service in the Luftwaffe. Dive-bombing was his unit's specialty. One day, Schneider was in Nazi-occupied Poland, walking through a town. There he witnessed some storm troopers murdering Jews in a synagogue's courtyard. Schneider particularly noticed that the rabbi died clutching the Torah.

The incident changed Schneider's life. He started to disobey orders. He dropped bombs on uninhabited areas. He adjusted detonators so that his bombs wouldn't explode. When World War II ended, Schneider vowed to do penance for twenty years. He went to work in coal mines, anonymously donating two-thirds of his salary to organizations aiding war orphans and survivors of the concentration camps. He taught himself Hebrew, and, taking a new name, he began to attend synagogue services.

After the twenty years, Schneider sold his farm and moved to Israel. He approached religious authorities about becoming a Jew. The authorities, at first not believing his story, investigated. When they realized he was telling the truth, they considered his past and what he had done since and accepted his application. Taking the name Reuel Abraham, he became both a Jew and a citizen of Israel.

Some converts were famous, but even their Jewish stories, their contributions to the Jewish people, are not widely known. For example, Elizabeth Taylor was one of the most prominent film actresses in the world. Many people familiar with Taylor's becoming Jewish incorrectly assume that she did so because of her marriage to Jewish film producer Mike Todd. However, it was almost a year after Todd died in an airplane crash that Taylor undertook a ceremony at Temple Israel in Hollywood. On March 27, 1959, the twenty-seven-year-old world-famous star took the Hebrew name Elisheba Rachel and embraced Judaism. She did so because she was attracted to the Jewish heritage. She told one of her biographers that she identified with the Jews as underdogs.

She made many contributions to Jewish life. Not long after her conversion she purchased so many Israel bonds that Arab countries boycotted her films. In 1967 she cancelled a trip to Moscow to protest the USSR's condemnation of Israel's actions during the Six-Day War. She signed a letter denouncing the UN's "Zionism is racism" resolution. In 1976 she offered to exchange places with a hostage held by Palestine Liberation Organization hijackers.

It is because of people like these and the untold numbers of those who voluntarily embraced Judaism through the ages and made great sacrifices and great contributions that the Jewish people should actively welcome converts. This book explains the benefits converts bring, the stories they have to tell, the unfair resistance they face from some in the Jewish world, and the controversies they engender.

What is perhaps most amazing in the tale of converts to Judaism is how little known they are among born Jews, how unfamiliar many in the Jewish community are with their history, the reasons why Jews at one point in their history actively sought converts, and why persecution forced them to stop welcoming those who wanted to become Jewish.

It is important to tell their stories, to inform the Jewish public of their presence, to alert born Jews to a history that is almost hidden, and to provide role models for those who might wish to join the Jewish people on their historic spiritual journey. Those potential converts need to know that they have many companions in history. The role models are crucial so that those considering conversion and those who have converted will see that they are part of a great story, that their decision to attach their fate to that of the Jewish people is noble and deeply rooted in Jewish religious traditions. The role models, though, also provide a crucial lesson for those born Jewish. Many born Jews think of conversion only in the context of intermarriage, whereas in fact conversion has a wide and deep history apart from romantic attachments.

Born Jews who incorrectly believe that converts aren't genuine Jews will be surprised and enlightened when they discover the range of those who have become Jewish.

The story of converts must begin with defining the key concepts being discussed. Conversion to Judaism (in Hebrew the term is *giyur*) is a legal act undertaken by someone who is not born Jewish according to Jewish law or accepted as Jewish by the community in which the person lives. This act is meant to allow the person to be considered as Jewish by the Jewish community. The word *giyur* was not a religious word originally. It meant naturalization, or becoming part of the Jewish people, not joining the Jewish religion. Of course, those who joined the people were seen as part of a religious people.

The person undergoing the conversion is called a convert. The Hebrew word for a convert is *ger* (male, plural *gerim*) or *givoret* (female). The word *ger* is derived from the Hebrew verb *l'gar*, which means "to reside." The *ger* in the Hebrew Bible describes a foreigner who lived among the Israelites. The Greek translation of the Bible uses the new word "proselyte" to refer to a *ger*. By Rabbinic times the word had taken on a more religious meaning and meant a specifically religious convert to Judaism. Some converts to Judaism understandably and justifiably don't like to be called a "convert." Indeed, by Jewish law they are, with some exceptions, fully Jewish and should not be put in a separate group. But to understand the phenomenon of conversion it is necessary to define converts using the term while at the same time acknowledging that they have no inferior status as Jews. The term "convert" in this book is used historically and sociologically, and its use should be understood as not in any way questioning or denigrating those who become Jewish. Additionally, some object to the word "convert" as sounding Christian, not Jewish. Some people therefore apply other terms to a convert, such as a "Jew by choice" or "new Jew." The problem with "proselyte" or one of these new terms, however, is that those terms are not widely understood, whereas the word "convert" has widespread understanding.

Whatever word is used to describe the convert, though, the seemingly simple definition of conversion is fraught with complexities.

For example, according to traditional Jewish law as it eventually developed, only people who are born to a Jewish mother are considered legally Jewish. (It should be noted that this matrilineal principle had to develop and was not part of Jewish beliefs from the beginning of the faith). But the Reform movement, among other liberal denominations, accepts the patrilineal principle, by which someone is considered Jewish who does not have a Jewish mother but has a Jewish father and was raised exclusively as Jewish. Patrilineal Jews are not accepted as legally Jewish by, for example, Orthodox and Conservative Jews. As if that's not problem enough, the difficulties multiply exponentially when issues of conversion are considered. For example, some Orthodox and other rabbis do not recognize any conversions performed by non-Orthodox rabbis. Indeed, some Orthodox rabbis in Israel don't recognize the conversions of some Orthodox American rabbis. There is no agreed-upon curriculum for potential converts to study. There is no agreement about the specific requirements for conversion.

These intense and complicated religious struggles have resulted in some odd situations. Consider, for example, the case of Yisrael Campbell, an Israeli comedian who appeared in the off-Broadway show and documentary titled *Circumcise Me*. Born Christopher Campbell in Philadelphia to an ex-nun and a schoolteacher, the comedian uses his family as part of his repertoire. For example, the bearded, black-hatted, sidecurl-wearing comic notes that his aunt is still a nun. And so, he notes, that "makes Jesus my uncle, allowing for easier parking in Jerusalem." After a troubled youth, Campbell underwent a Reform conversion. But his spiritual search continued, and so he wanted additional recognition. He therefore sought a second conversion with a Conservative rabbi. In 2000, he spent four months in Israel, a trip that convinced him to lead an Orthodox life. He therefore underwent a third conversion and today lives in Jerusalem.

The act of bringing Gentiles to Judaism also has no clear term. In Christian religious discourse, the words "missionary work" refer clearly to the idea of seeking converts and may include such actions as going overseas to seek international converts and, in some cases, specific actions such as knocking on people's doors to interest them in the religion.

Jewish efforts to absorb new converts generally avoid words like "missionary work" precisely because they are associated with other religions and because sometimes harsh and even deadly efforts have been made in the past to force Jewish conversions to other religions. The more general word "mission," referring to a purpose of religious life, can be used, but even this is rare and is resisted. It should be noted, though, that embracing converts can be seen as part of Judaism's religious obligations.

Jewish efforts are not even seen as seeking converts, for that is an active task, whereas most converts to Judaism come to the faith and the people on their own. Still, there are some more active efforts, and so a term is needed to cover both active and passive Jewish efforts to accept newcomers to their religion.

The term "welcoming" is used in this book. The word is meant to be flexibly applied and can refer to placing ads in papers providing information about conversion classes, or placing announcements in congregational bulletins that a rabbi will help teach converts, or simply agreeing to teach potential converts who come to a rabbi on their own, with no Jewish outreach.

"Welcoming" is meant to convey that all these and other related efforts are done without coercion, or force, or emotional blackmail, or pressure and without intruding on the privacy of others such as by stopping people in a public place or making an unsolicited call or visit to their home. The book will chart the ways such Jewish welcoming developed and how it might evolve in the future.

And it should be clear that just as there are disputes about who can conduct a conversion and what is required of people who wish to become Jewish, so, too, is there sometimes emotional upheaval and a less-than-welcoming attitude toward converts.

When I was doing research for my guidebook for converts, I heard from a woman with such a story. I called the couple Sam and Cathy. Sam's parents were Jewish; Cathy's were Protestant. Both sets of parents were vehemently opposed to the match. Sam's parents offered him $10,000 if he forgot Cathy. He was shocked, and then he angrily refused the offer. His parents then said they would accept Cathy if Sam went to Israel for two years and studied with a rabbi. Again, Sam refused, but his parents persisted and, seeing a way to win their ultimate acceptance, he discussed the suggestion with Cathy. They agreed to Sam's going to Israel.

Sam sat on the airplane to Israel and wrote Cathy a letter. When he arrived, he began a regular routine of writing letters telling her about his activities. But Sam was stunned. Cathy never answered his letters. Confused, he wrote to his parents and asked them to investigate. They agreed, though they said they could not discover the reason she didn't write.

A frustrated Sam returned to the United States after two months, but when he got to Cathy's house, her parents told him she was on a trip to Europe. He left several letters with them, but Cathy never replied.

It was several months later that Cathy's parents wrote him. They said that Cathy had married an old friend and hinted that she was expecting a child. Sam flew back to see Cathy but instead had an angry confrontation with her father. The police had to be called.

Confused and dazed, Sam returned again to Israel. His landlady, an older woman with three children, tried to get him interested in her. Sam was desperately unhappy. He wondered what had happened to Cathy.

If only he had known. Cathy's parents had suggested a trip to Europe to take her mind off Sam's absence. It sounded like a great idea, and she agreed. She waited for Sam's letters, but her parents told her that he had never written. Eventually they told her that Sam had gotten married in Israel. Cathy rushed to Sam's parents, who confirmed that he was married and very happy in his new life.

Cathy got married, but the partnership lasted only four months before the annulment.

Four years passed since Cathy had dropped Sam at the airport for his trip. And then one day her telephone rang. Sam's sister was calling. The truth came pouring out. Sam was returning. He had written more than fifty letters and been told that Cathy did not even want to read them. He wasn't really married. His parents had told him that Cathy was married with two children.

Sam's sister said she would bring her brother directly from the airport to see Cathy. The sister said she would inform him of the truth.

Sam arrived, and the two spent their first hour just hugging. Then they spoke at great length about what had happened.

Eventually, Cathy told Sam a secret. Two weeks after he first left for Israel she had begun her secret conversion to Judaism.

Few conversion stories have such extended drama, but many of the stories are filled with deep and abiding love and devotion to the Jewish faith. They are stories worth telling and worth hearing.

There are a wide variety of reasons why people convert to Judaism. Some begin with a romantic attachment to someone

Jewish, though it should be noted that such relationships don't cause conversions because people can get married without any conversion. Usually, the relationship provokes an interest in Judaism, and as studying progresses, the interest deepens. Sometimes people don't convert until after a marriage, frequently when a child is born. But there are many motivations of people who become Jewish.

There are, for example, a variety of spiritual reasons. Judaism's worldview, its sense of ethics, and its values are seen as worth embracing. Some people enjoy the religious services or the various Jewish customs and practices such as the seder at Passover or the Hanukkah candle lighting. There are, of course, romantic reasons as well, such as sharing a love's religion or the knowledge that the children of a marriage would have a Jewish identity. There are communal reasons, such as that Jews have a warm community worth joining. Finally, there are personal reasons, such as seeing joining a new religion as exciting.

These positive reasons, though, are sometimes balanced with emotional difficulties. Some converts feel the loss of a previous identity. Many, understandably, feel a sense of being overwhelmed with new information and new expectations as well as exciting, conflicting, and confusing feelings. Some feel marginal, as though they no longer belong to their previous religious identity but aren't accepted as fully Jewish.

Going through the conversion process is not easy. As discussed, there is not even an agreed-upon process among and sometimes within the various Jewish denominations. Here is a description of a process that includes steps that may or may not be in a particular individual's process. The list is meant to be inclusive.

That process starts with a potential convert's decision to explore Judaism. An introduction to Judaism or conversion class does not obligate a person to complete the conversion. Usually, the decision involves reading, talking with family and friends and a loved one if appropriate, and eventually approaching a rabbi to serve as a guide to the process. The rabbi is first concerned about a potential person's sincerity. Indeed, some rabbis adhere to the Jewish tradition of turning a convert away to test that sincerity.

If the rabbi and the potential convert agree to continue, the next step is to study Judaism. It is common at this stage to participate in Jewish life, to attend synagogue, to experience home rituals, such as those observed on Shabbat, the Sabbath, and to study either with the rabbi or in a class. Such study might include elementary Hebrew, Jewish holidays, history, and observances, and the Jewish family. A typical course might meet weekly for six months or a year (and so the need to plan in advance if a couple wants a Jewish wedding in which both partners participate as Jews). Some converts feel these classes lean too much to the intellectual side and not enough to the experiential. Such converts want not only to learn about Shabbat but to be shown how to say the prayers, for example.

There are conversion classes available online, such as on YouTube and by individual rabbis, though many converts prefer more traditional means so that they can have human interaction with the rabbi and other students.

After the period of study, the candidate is ready for the *bet din*. The religious court typically consists of three people, at least one of whom is a rabbi. The *bet din* has many purposes. There are substantive questions about Judaism so that the convert has a chance to display knowledge acquired. For example, there might be a question about the Jewish belief in one God. These questions are not meant to be traps. Members of the *bet din* understand that candidates are nervous. The *bet din* will also want to know that the convert is sincere about the conversion, that there has been no pressure applied to become Jewish, and that the candidate genuinely wants to join the Jewish people. Sometimes an oath of allegiance to the Jewish people is signed.

For males, Orthodox, Conservative, and some Reform rabbis require a circumcision, or *brit milah*. This rite is biblically based and signifies the entry into the covenant with God. The word *brit* in fact means "covenant." In cases, for example, when the male has already undergone a circumcision, a drop of blood is symbolically drawn in a ceremony known as *hatafat dam brit*.

Orthodox, Conservative, and some Reform rabbis require both male and female candidates for conversion to immerse themselves in a *mikveh*, a ritual bath. The immersion symbolically makes the candidate ritually clean to enter Judaism and represents the candidate's total commitment to the new religion and the rebirth of the person as a Jew. Any body of natural water can be a *mikveh*, but there are also specific pools that are built just for ritual purification. Such a *mikveh* might, for example, be located in a house of worship, or a Jewish community center, or a separate building. The ceremony typically consists of a shower and a covering of the candidate that is removed when entering the *mikveh*'s warm water (when the immersion ceremony is done in a public place, the candidate wears a loose-fitting garment). Candidates immerse themselves and say the appropriate blessings. In more traditional *mikveh* ceremonies, a woman attendant tells three males outside, who are the required legal witnesses, that the blessings have been said. This allows for appropriate modesty.

In ancient times it was traditional to bring an offering to the Temple as part of the conversion process. This ceremony ended after the Temple's second destruction in the year 70 CE (Common Era). Some traditional rabbis suggest that a symbolic offering be made, though such an act is not part of Jewish law. Some possible offerings include donating money to the poor or engaging in some other act of charity.

The next step is to choose a Hebrew name. Sometimes this is done at the *bet din*, but there are a variety of possibilities, depending on the particular case. The Hebrew name is needed so that the new Jew will be able to be part of future religious ceremonies, such as a marriage. The new name is meant to symbolize a new birth, a new life. By tradition, a Hebrew name consists of a first name (and perhaps a second or third) and then a parental name, such as Shimon ben Eliezer, or "Shimon, the son of Eliezer." The convert may not have a Jewish parent, so the name ben Avraham Avinu, meaning "the son of Abraham, our father," is chosen. For women, the convert might be named bat Sarah Imenu, "the daughter of Sarah, our mother." Increasingly, a person is called the child of both parents, so that in contemporary usage a person might be named Shimon ben Eliezer v' Devorah, "Shimon the son of Eliezer and Deborah."

In some cases, the process of becoming Jewish is completed by a public ceremony. Perhaps, for example, a convert stands in front of a congregation and gives a speech about becoming Jewish or participates in a graduation ceremony. Some converts do not want a public ceremony. They might not, for instance, like to be singled out as converts rather than be considered as simply Jewish. But many converts enjoy such a ceremony. After all, it gives them a chance to thank their family, friends, rabbi, teachers, and others who helped them. Such stories often help born Jews.

The story of how Jewish laws, rituals, and ceremonies about conversion evolved is part of this book's scope. The Reform alternative to Jewish law will also be explored. It is quite a story.

That story of how these rituals developed is only one of the questions the book will answer. We will explore the amazing stories of individuals and groups who became Jewish and ask why they did. Why did Jews want to welcome them? And why do many Jews believe that Judaism never welcomed converts and should be very reluctant to do so now? We will explore what is at stake in the controversies surrounding conversion, what effect Israel's intense debates about conversion have on converts in the United States and elsewhere, the nature of welcoming converts as a Jewish religious obligation, the role of conversion in the ongoing discussions about interfaith marriages, and other topics.

We will consider the arguments used against welcoming converts and why those arguments are deficient. In a way, the story of the converts and the laws and all else covered in the book is meant as a description of the benefits that converts bring the Jewish people and so as reasons why Jews should welcome converts. Some of these reasons are not so obvious. Judaism is not a commercial product; seeing it as comparable provides an important clue to one reason why converts help born Jews. Consider any product, say, a healthful food product. When advertisers put on commercials they have two goals. One is to get new customers to buy the product. But another goal is to convince current customers that they should stick with the product and not switch to a competitor. In so commercial a country as the United States, with a large number of people switching religions, each religion is comparable to that product. When Judaism wins new members, the choice of people to convert to Judaism brings many benefits, but perhaps the most hidden one is that such conversions subtly convince born Jews that they have made a good choice to remain as Jews.

The sources for the book include all the basic Jewish foundational texts, including the Hebrew Bible and the Talmud. Additionally, as the list of resources in the References section makes clear, there is an enormous amount of research available about conversion. I've read more books and articles than I listed in that section, but those additional sources primarily provided background and amplification rather than new materials. Finally, I contacted many rabbis, scholars, and research institutions to make sure I did not overlook some perhaps forgotten but nonetheless important figure. The book is not a complete history; there are always more tales to tell. But I meant to provide (and hope I have provided) a coherent story profiling the major figures and telling the central story of the too-often-neglected tale of converts in Jewish history.

The story told in this book begins at the very beginning of the Jewish people. One of the Bible's many interesting curiosities is that its story does not begin with the first person on earth being Jewish. Rather, the Bible tells how the Jewish people began with the staggering religious insights of a single man, the crucial support of his wife, and the miracle that led to the emergence of a still unfinished spiritual odyssey.

1

YOUR PEOPLE SHALL BE MY PEOPLE

Converts in the Biblical Era

Abraham, as the founder of the Jewish people, is the first convert to Judaism. Almost all the words in that sentence, though, need to be clarified. There was no religious conversion at the time of Abraham if conversion is correctly defined as a legal act making a Gentile person into someone Jewish. There was also no Judaism, if "Judaism" is understood in the modern sense of the word as a religion. Indeed "Judaism" is only a term used in modernity, not even applicable at all to the biblical Israelites or several later historical Jewish periods. And those are not the only problems with the sentence. Abraham may be a real historical figure, or he may be a creation of the person who wrote his story for the biblical text. It is not even clear what it means to talk about the "Jewish people."

Still, with all these complications, the basic idea of Abraham as the first convert makes sense. Abraham, originally named Abram (meaning "the father is exalted"), was born in Babylonia in the city of Ur of the Chaldees, in southern Mesopotamia, perhaps around 1800 BCE (Before the Common Era). Tradition puts the date at 1812 BCE. The family moved to Haran, in northwestern Mesopotamia. Abram's father, Terah, was a pagan who sold idols.

Abram came to the overwhelming spiritual insight that the cosmos was not controlled by many gods but by a single God. As such, Abram was the father of monotheism, the belief in one God.

It was a blinding, life-altering insight, a sudden reconfiguration of reality. But Abram's transformation was not over. In a defining moment of human history, after Terah's death, God called out to Abram with a divine plan. Abram was to leave his family and his home and journey to Canaan, what is now called Eretz Yisrael, the "Land of Israel," where he and his descendants would become a great nation. In return, God promised that Abram would be the father of many nations (the meaning of the name "Abraham") and a blessing for all of the earth's families. Abram accepted this covenant (a contract or agreement that in Hebrew is called a *brit*) and permanently symbolized it in Jewish life by the ritual of circumcision (called a *brit milah*—a covenant of circumcision).

Whether or not Abraham was a real person, the symbolic nature of his theological observations, of his relationship with the one God, of his becoming a moral partner with that God, perfectly reflect the core Jewish apprehensions of human existence. Abraham converted to a new reality, and that is the heart of the conversion experience and the model for all future converts.

Abram began his journey with Sarai (later Sarah), his wife. She was, again symbolically, the second convert to Judaism. Abram also brought his nephew, Lot. This new people, inaccurately but still usefully called the Jewish people, that is, started with Abram's family members. Even now, many conversions in all religions occur because of a family attachment.

Abram and Sarai's historic move to Canaan to found a new people, a new nation, included the souls (*nefesh*) they had gathered in Haran (Genesis 12:5). In later tradition, rabbis during the Talmudic era concluded that these souls included the male and female converts Abram and Sarai had acquired as they convinced others that one God existed and that it was required that they be faithful to that God. Even now, while there is no legal mandate requiring them to do so, many male converts accept the Hebrew name of Avraham ben Avraham Avinu (Abraham, the son of Abraham, our father), and women converts often choose the name Sarah bat Avraham Avinu (Sarah, the daughter of Abraham, our father).

The crucial fact, apart from the historic accuracy of the text, is the vital notion that someone not born to an Israelite family could join it as could someone who did not previously believe in one God. That is, in more contemporary language, in theory a Gentile could become Jewish. Conversion was to be allowed. Abraham's son Isaac and grandson Jacob married such Gentiles who joined the Jewish people. This notion in the Torah (the sacred first five books of the Hebrew Bible) is made clear by the fact that, for example, Zipporah, the wife of Moses, the most important figure in the religious history of the Jewish people, was the daughter of Jethro, a priest from Midian and himself a convert. David, the great king and from whose line the Messiah would one day arrive, was the great-grandson of Ruth (perhaps the most famous convert in the Bible) and the husband of Maacah, the daughter of Talmai, the king of Geshur and the mother of Absalom. Solomon's son Rehoboam, the successor of the throne of Judea, had Naamah the Ammonite as a mother. Over and over again, that is, the irreplaceable leaders of the Jewish people were themselves converts, descended from converts, or married to converts. Indeed, in a crucial sense because Abraham and Sarah were converts, traced back far enough every single member of the Jewish people had an ancestor who was a convert.

Abraham is called an Ivri, or Hebrew, and so his people were called Hebrews. The word "Hebrew" may refer to Abraham's ancestor Eber or perhaps to his arrival from the other side (*eber*) of the Eurphrates River. Abraham's grandson, Jacob, whom God renames "Israel," means, in one translation, one who wrestles with God. The Israelites are, then, descendants of Jacob. It is vital to note that an Israelite is not someone who "believes" in God but someone who struggles with the reality of God. Judaism is not, that is, a confessional religion requiring adherence to a constructed set of beliefs. Rather, it may more usefully be thought of as a people who believe it is crucial to think about one's relationship with God. Later, much more traditional definitions would emerge, with commandments, but at its beginnings, the Jewish people were a confederation of people who acted very much like a tribe that banded together for communal self-defense and mutual support. People were allowed to enter this tribe without having to swear to a prescribed set of beliefs.

The Israelites, that is, were an ethnic group, or tribe, or people. They were not a religion. There was no separation of a people and their religion. The words Jew and Judaism were nonexistent. People "converted" not to Judaism but became part of the people by attaching themselves to the group, primarily through marriage or the acceptance of the beliefs of the Israelites. There were many non-Israelites who, in this loose sense of the word, converted through assimilation into the people.

Again according to tradition, the Israelites were enslaved in Egypt and escaped during the Exodus, making their way to Mount Sinai, where they received the Torah and made a covenant with God as a people. They journeyed then to Canaan, where they entered the land. While there is no direct archaeological evidence of the Exodus, the size of which is described in the Bible, this master story of the role of Moses, who led the Exodus, received the Torah, and became the founder of the religion of Judaism, is beyond the realm of history. Its truth is independent of fact, for it was believed for thousands of years and shaped all of the Jewish future.

The story of the Exodus has Israelites leaving Egypt with a "mixed multitude" (Exodus 12:38). There is a variety of suggestions about who made up that mixed multitude, from mercenaries to Egyptians who had intermarried with the Israelites. However the words are interpreted, the crucial point is that once again the Israelites saw it as acceptable to increase their numbers by absorbing people who were not born into their existing group. Again, loosely used, "converts" were accepted as a natural part of Israelite life.

After their return to the Land of Israel from Egypt, the Israelites gained new members of their people from among the people in Canaan. (One nonbiblical theory is that there was no Exodus, no sojourn in Egypt, and that the Israelites arose from native Canaanites. This historical debate is outside the book's scope.) Those native Canaanites included the Hittites, Hivvites, Girgashites, Amorites, Perizzites, Jesusites, and others.

Of course, not all the foreigners in the land of Canaan became part of the Israelite people in the land (the *ezrach*). Legally, the foreigners were divided into two groups. A foreigner could be a *ger*, a resident alien who lived in the land more or less permanently, or foreigners (*zarim* or *nokhrim*) who were only visiting the land or staying there temporarily. These foreigners came to the land for various reasons, sometimes as invaders but more commonly for commercial reasons. These foreigners were not subject to the laws of the Israelites, but they were to be treated well because it was a religious obligation to treat strangers well.

The *ger* was characteristically a permanent resident of the land. It was only after their experience of slavery in Egypt that the Israelites created the class of *gerim*, recognizing that they themselves had been strangers or aliens. Once in Canaan, the Israelites attracted native Canaanites and new immigrants to the land—people, for example, who searched in Canaan for relief from famine or drought elsewhere or who sought to escape during a military action.

The *gerim* mostly did everyday labor. But it was their poverty and vulnerability that served as constant reminders of their weakness and the Israelite obligation to treat them well, to give them fair legal treatment, to treat the Israelite and the stranger in the same way.

The ways of assimilation worked over time, and many *gerim* became absorbed into the Israelite people. It was in fact common for pagan women who married Israelite men to adopt their clan and in so doing also adopt their religious views. These marriages were seen as positive because paganism was seen as idolatry, and marriage and adoption of the Torah meant that the pagans were brought to God. There are some specific examples named in the Bible. These include Doeg the Edomite (1 Samuel 21:8) and Uriah the Hittite (2 Samuel 11:11). The *gerim*, unlike the *nokhrim*, had to follow the ritual and religious laws of the land, such as observing the Sabbath and various festivals. They were required to fast on Yom Kippur.

There were not rigid differences between the two groups as social classes. An Israelite might be a poor laborer and a *ger* a successful landowner. It was unsurprising, then, that members of the two groups met, mixed, and married.

The Bible has numerous references to the gaining of converts to Judaism: Ezra 2:59–60, Ezra 6:21, Nehemiah 10:29 ("and everyone who withdrew from the uncleanness of the peoples of the lands to the teaching of God").

There was, over time, a linguistic transformation. By the time of the Second Temple (516 BCE–70 CE) the term *ger* referred specifically to a convert.

It should be noted that there was another legal designation. The *ger* can be understood as the resident stranger who became an Israelite through conversion. The *ger toshav*, or resident stranger, accepted some of the Torah's commandments but not all. The *ger toshav*, that is, was not a convert to Judaism and, while allowed to live in the Land of Israel, was not part of the Israelite people. The status of the *ger toshav* would evolve in later religious writing, as we shall see.

The impulse to attract converts depended in part on the evolving Israelite understanding of God. In the beginning of Israelite thought about God, the deity was a national one, protecting the Israelites in their native land, helping them as they fought, protecting them from hunger and illness. Sacrifices to this God were crucial because such sacrifices could stave off various misfortunes such as illness or bad crops. God, that is, was God exclusively of the Israelites. They were not allowed to worship other deities, and God protected them exclusively. It should be noted, however, that there were alternate religious views among some Israelites. In the eighth century BCE (and even earlier in some cases), some of the Israelites sought protection from Asherah, a supposed goddess married to the Hebrew God. That is, monotheism did not develop all at once but evolved over time and not without internal struggles.

There is no impulse to encourage other people to become an Israelite within this religious view. But this concept began to change in the 800s BCE. The Assyrians desired control over the entire world. This military and political goal engendered the idea of a single and unified world. The Israelites characteristically applied a spiritual interpretation to the Assyrian view. The prophet Amos (c. 751 BCE), for example, asserted that the God the Israelites worshipped was not just the God of the one people but also the God of all humanity, of all the world. Amos also drew the connection between the observance of the commandments (the *mitzvot*) and God's fidelity to the covenant established at Mount Sinai. God was separate from the Israelite people and could withdraw the covenant and offer it to another people if the Israelites were not faithful to the commandments.

If Amos can be called the first universalist, that does not mean he fully comprehended the implications of his views. He thought, for example, that God could only enter into covenants serially, with one people or another, but not with all people. There were no simultaneous covenants for Amos. Nor was there the idea that the Israelites could worship God outside the Land of Israel.

The biggest advance to the idea of a world God, to the notion that all people should worship that world God, came from Amos's disciple Isaiah (c. 740–700 BCE). Isaiah also focused on Assyrian power and how to interpret it. He concluded that Assyria, no less than the Israelites, was subject to God's ethical injunctions. This was a crucial intellectual step forward.

In Genesis, all humans were seen as part of a single family tracing their roots back to Adam and Eve. It was Isaiah who connected the notion of collective humanity to the idea of unity through the teachings of the Torah. In Isaiah 2:2 and following, Isaiah makes a prophecy that all nations will go to seek instruction from God, from the revelation that has emerged from Jerusalem, from God's holy word. This vision is shared by another prophet, Micah (Micah 4:1ff), who was a contemporary of Isaiah. But it was Isaiah with the clearest vision of converts. In 14:1 Isaiah foresees a time when *gerim* will come and attach themselves to the house of Israel.

The Babylonian destruction of the First Temple in Jerusalem in 586 BCE and the subsequent exile of the Israelites to Babylon, where they were captives, had history-altering effects. The exile first of all destroyed the existing political structure, the tribal alignment, that existed. In severing the national identity of the people now apart from their sacred land, the exile inevitably made them focus on the other key components: their shared history and especially their religion. A national people became a religious people. The priesthood, based on lineage, no longer was central because there was no Temple for priests to lead. Rabbis, focusing on religious scholarship and rewarded on the basis of their learning, replaced the priests. The destroyed Temple was replaced by synagogues and academies. The sacrifices in the Temple were replaced by prayer and study of the Torah.

The prophet Jeremiah arose and made a revolutionary contribution to Israelite thinking about God. Jeremiah argued that God could be worshipped outside the Land of Israel. In principle, that is, the God of all people could be worshipped anywhere in the world. It might seem that such a change only affected the Israelites, providing the necessary insight to allow them to pray wherever they were. But in terms of conversion to Judaism, Jeremiah's assertion is also vital. For the insight changed the view of Gentiles. Israelites could now worship a portable God, and Gentiles living anywhere could join the Israelite people, could accept God without having to move to the Land of Israel but simply by accepting the necessary religious views.

Exile changed the idea of being a *ger* in the same way. A stranger could not join the Israelite nation because there was no longer a nation to join. *Gerim* were now understood not as people who attached themselves to the Israelites in the land but as people who attached themselves to God. Those Gentiles who engaged in such an attachment to God were called *nilvim* (Isaiah 14:1, 56:3, 56:6; Esther 9:27; Zechariah 2:15) or *nivdalim*, people who had left the Gentile world to adhere to the sacred Israelite law (Ezra 6:21).

The theological conclusion was now in place: every Gentile in every land could worship God. The connections were in place. God had given the Torah to the Israelites at Mount Sinai. Everyone, anywhere, could join the Israelites in adhering to the Torah. The prophet Ezekiel's conclusion that God wished to be worshipped by all people combined with the conclusion that idolatry was a sin. The Israelites were moving step by step toward the final conclusion that it was a religious obligation to offer their religion to everyone in the world.

The next stop on the trail toward this conclusion was the belief that God punished sins. There was a view that God's vision was one of moral justice, that humans would be judged, and that evil would be punished. This moral calculus led to the notion that idolatry was unacceptable, that those who followed idols were sinning. This conclusion provided a powerful impulse to confront idolaters, to provide them with a path to God.

It was Isaiah who provided the final step to the Israelites' understanding of encouraging conversion as their obligatory religious mission. Isaiah asks an obvious question: Who was it that would teach pagans about God? Who would impart divine truth? Who would offer the moral laws to the nations? Who would rescue humanity from any Godly retribution? To ask the questions was to answer them, for it was obvious. The people of Israel were the divine messengers. They had the word of God. All could accept it. The Israelites would be the moral teachers for all humanity. God had toughened them through exile. They would return to their land and offer God's revelation to humanity. And they would do so with an act, the striking act of religious conversion. Indeed, in Isaiah 56:1–8 the very idea of religious conversion is introduced. Isaiah, speaking in the language of his day, talks about burnt offerings and sacrifices. Isaiah notes that God's house shall be "a house of prayer for all peoples." This explicit call to bring all people to God is a clear pronouncement of the Israelite mission.

Given this history, it is not surprising that on Rosh Hashanah in 516 BCE—that is, at the ceremony of the dedication of the Second Temple built when the Israelites returned from Babylonia—the prophet Zechariah proclaimed a program to encourage and seek converts to Judaism (Zechariah 8:20–23). This effort to seek converts commenced.

It was interrupted in 458 BCE when Ezra returned from Babylonia and was later helped by Nehemiah, who returned in 444 BCE. They railed against the rampant intermarriages and saw Judaism as particularist, not universal. It is possible that the Book of Ruth, set in the eleventh century BCE, was written in reaction to the particularist legislation in 458 BCE (mentioned in Ezekiel 44:6–9).

Ruth is the most famous convert to Judaism in the Bible. Ruth, a Moabite, married Mahlon, a man from Judea whose family had come to Moab to escape a famine in Bethlehem. (Although not part of the story, the writer of this biblical book had a great deal of fun with language. Ironically, for example, Bethlehem means "the food house." All the names have clear symbolic meanings as well. Ruth, for example, means "the companion.") After Mahlon and his brother die, their mother, Naomi, decides to return to Bethlehem. Naomi tells her widowed daughters-in-law to return to their own mothers and remarry. One, named Orpah, reluctantly departs. But Ruth says (Ruth 1:16), "Wherever you go, I will go; wherever you lodge, I will lodge; your people shall be my people, and your God my God." It is not known whether these words were spoken spontaneously by Ruth (that is, invented by the writer) or whether they were part of an existing conversion ceremony. By the time of the Talmud (Yevamoth 47b), Ruth's words were understood to mean that she had embraced Judaism. In more contemporary times, the words have been incorporated into conversion ceremonies for many Jewish women.

Ruth remarried and had a son, Obed, who is the father of Jesse, who in turn had his own son, King David. This is the lineage through which Ruth becomes, according to tradition, the ancestor of the Messiah.

The attachment of non-Israelites to the Israelite people came about through natural means in the biblical period. Foreign wives, slaves, people who came to the land for commercial opportunities, and others entered into the orbit of and were absorbed by the Israelites. But the next stage in conversion, the more active efforts to encourage conversion rather than passively accept it when it occurred, was about to take place.

And that started with Alexander the Great.

2

OVER LAND AND SEA

The Rise of Proselytism in the Hellenistic and Early
Roman Period

This chapter covers the years from Alexander the Great in 336 BCE to the Bar Kokhba rebellion against Roman rule in the year 135 CE, a tumultuous era in Jewish history. It was an era that began with Alexander's conquests. But when it comes to conversion, the real story is not Alexander the Great's military conquests but the conquests of Greek ideas. The Hellenistic philosophy of the Greeks had an enormous influence in the Jewish world, especially in Alexandria. It was during this time that the Septuagint, the Greek translation of the Hebrew Bible, was completed, as we'll see below. In Jewish philosophy the era gave rise to Philo, who sought to find a synthesis between Jewish thought and Greek philosophy.

This may all seem like simple ancient history, but as William Faulkner once wrote (in his 1951 novel *Requiem for a Nun*), "The past isn't dead. It isn't even past." This assertion certainly applies to the Hellenistic and early Roman period because there are at least two principal ongoing debates about the era, one of which has profound contemporary political reverberations.

The first controversy extends beyond the era but starts during it. This controversy focuses on a thesis propounded most recently by the Israeli historian Shlomo Sand. In his 2009 book *The Invention of the Jewish People*, Sand argues that most contemporary Ashkenazi Jews (who, for example, make up about 90 percent of American Jews) are the descendants not of the ancient Israelites but of converts (including the Khazars, a subject to be discussed in a later chapter). The idea of the Jewish people, that is, was invented. Sand's purpose was to argue that Zionists could not legitimately claim that Jews had a right to the land based on their ancestors' history. He seeks, that is, to undermine the moral legitimacy of Israel.

It should be noted that most historians and most geneticists dismiss Sand's argument as false. Dr. Harry Ostrer, a prominent medical geneticist, has shown in his book *Legacy: A Genetic History of the Jewish People* that Jews from a variety of groups in the Diaspora share genetic threads that link them together biologically and that these Jews have a Semitic ancestry originating in the Middle East and are more related to each other than to groups of Gentiles. Sand, then, is inaccurate, but confusion arises because Jews have a mixed descent. There were genetic variations within Jewish groups precisely because Judaism was so active a proselytizing religion, and so every Jewish group in antiquity was in part created because converts joined that people. Therefore, as Ostrer points out, European Jews had mixed European and Middle Eastern ancestry, and North African Jews had some significant North African ancestry. What this all shows is that Jews are of Middle Eastern origin but that they spread out all over the Roman and Persian Empires, a conclusion amply borne out by archaeological evidence. Some estimates are that only 10 percent of Jews were living in Judea. As they spread out, they gained converts who mixed with the Jews. Therefore, while Sand is correct that there was widespread acceptance of converts, that does not undermine the connection between the Jews of today and ancient Israel.

Many Jews will be surprised to learn that some of their ancestors were converts or that at one time Jews actively sought to gain new adherents. The change in Jewish attitude will be part of the story as well.

The second controversy revolves around whether or not the Jews were an active missionary or proselytizing religion during this time, and, if so, what means they used to gain converts. This debate, one mostly limited to scholars, is somewhat based on language. History doesn't record the name of a Jewish missionary in the sense that Christians had missionaries. Part of the debate centers, that is, on whether Christianity inherited the idea of missionaries from Judaism or invented the notion. It is more precise to think of the Judeans (or Jews) as proselytizing—that is, seeking to convert people to Judaism. The word "proselyte" referring to a convert is Greek in origin. The word "proselyte" was used by the Greeks in their translation of the New Testament to translate the word *ger*, so a proselyte can be understood as a convert to Judaism.

As we shall see, if we understand that Jews did not have organized missionaries the way we understand the word through Christianity, that does not at all mean there was no effort by individuals and collectively to gain converts. We will learn about how merchants, Jewish refugees fleeing religious persecution and poverty, slaves, and other Jews wandered around the empires of the day spreading Judaism.

In this debate between those who argue that Judaism was an active missionary religion and those who don't, the demographic argument is key. Demography in ancient times is not an exact science. Salo Baron, the twentieth century's preeminent historian of the Jews, is often cited. Baron estimates that prior to their exile in 586 BCE, there were no more than 150,000 Jews in Judea. By the middle of the first century CE, however, the world's Jewish population, according to Baron, numbered eight million and constituted fully one-eighth of the Roman Empire. Even if this number is off by a wide margin, there still needs to be an explanation of the increase. Certainly, part of the reason is natural. Perhaps, as we have seen at other times in Jewish history, there were social, economic, and theological impulses to increase the number of children in the family. The Jews had good hygiene. They didn't practice birth control or infanticide. Food supplies were more abundant than they had previously been. Still, most historians find the increase compelling enough to seek another explanation, and the one most historians accept is that Jews increased their number through conversions. This does not offer proof of active proselytizing but only says that Jews welcomed large numbers of converts during the era.

The case for Judaism being an active proselytizing religion rests not just on the genetic and demographic evidence but on other matters as well, such as literary works that seem to have been produced for the purpose of encouraging converts. As with all these proconversionary observations, however, it is important to note that there are scholars—Scot McKnight and Martin Goodman are two of them—who offer caveats and doubts. Their work, included in the References section, can be read as a counterbalance to the assertions presented here and in other books, for example, the work of Louis Feldman.

Let us then turn to the supposed literary evidence.

The Letter of Aristeas, probably written in the first half of the second century BCE, was a letter written by Aristeas to his brother Philocrates. The letter offers an apology for Judaism and a defense of the Temple and the Septuagint, a Greek translation of the Hebrew Bible. Aristeas argues that Judaism's idea of God, its legal structure, and its overall wisdom all make it a religion that everyone should embrace. The idea of proselytizing arises in the letter (227) when Aristeas writes that Jews must show charity to their enemies so that they will change and adopt the proper religion.

The *Sibylline Oracles* were probably written in the middle of the second century BCE. Written in Greek hexameters, these oracular assertions were thought to have been made by Sibyls, who supposedly had access to the divine and could reveal eternal truths. The central truth revealed is that there is one God, and that God is the God of the Israelites.

There is an abundance of other literature of the time with similar intentions to bring people within the tent of Judaism. These works include the great historian Josephus's *Contra Apionem* (*Against Apion*), in which the author defended Judaism, seeing its long history in contrast to Greek thought. Josephus notes that the masses displayed great enthusiasm to share in Jewish practices (2.282). That is, proselytism was a widespread enough phenomenon to be recognized and recorded by the major Jewish historian of the era. Josephus compared the spread of Judaism to the spread of God in permeating the universe. Since Judaism viewed God as omnipresent, clearly Josephus thought Judaism was spreading, and should spread, throughout the entire world. Josephus even, with some exaggeration, sees Abraham's journey to Egypt as a missionary effort.

The great Hellenistic Jewish philosopher Philo also wrote pro-conversionary literature, such as the *Apologia hyper Ioudaion*, a work that no longer exists. In other works, Philo enjoins Jews to love converts (*De Virtutibus* 20, 103–4) and in the same work writes that converts are the dearest friends of the Jews. In still another work (*De Vita Mosis* 2.5.27), Philo notes his belief that Jews make up half of humanity. That is, he thought Jewish proselytizing efforts were highly successful.

Joseph and Aseneth is another work that some see (and others don't) as promoting a Jewish mission. The work is a romance that

seeks to complete the biblical story of Joseph and his marriage to
Aseneth (Genesis 41:45). The work's central question is how
prototypical a Jew as Joseph could marry a Gentile whose father
was a priest of On. The ultimate answer is that such a marriage
was allowed precisely because Aseneth converted to Judaism.
This work is a good example that illustrates the scholarly debate.
Joseph does not proselytize. He does not go to Aseneth in search
of a convert. It is their love that prompts the conversion, not some
missionary enterprise. The lesson for some scholars is, therefore,
that proselytes were welcome but that Jews did not seek them
out. Of course, there is no evidence either way about whether the
romance was used to promote conversions among women. (Evidently, many more women than men converted to Judaism, perhaps because there was no circumcision required.) The implica-
tion, though, that conversions were coincidental to romances is at
odds with some evidence. For example, as we shall see, there was
much resentment about efforts to win converts. Writers such as
Horace, Juvenal, and Tacitus talk about converts to Judaism but
never discuss romantic entanglements as the motivating factor for
a conversion.

Other writers, including Eupolemus, Demetrius, and Aristo-
buis created materials evidently used to proselytize. Indeed, the
Septuagint itself was translated from the Hebrew by Onkelos
(Aquila), who was himself a proselyte and very attuned to conversionary issues in that document, especially in his translation of the
book of Isaiah. It is certainly plausible to see the translation itself
as an example of literature used to convince pagans to join the
Jewish people.

As mentioned, besides demographic and literary evidence, the
Jewish proselytizing efforts can be inferred from the reaction to
them, the resentment they spurred. The most famous of the out-
bursts against Jewish proselytizing efforts can be read in the New
Testament (Matthew 23:15), in which the writer bitterly claims

that the Pharisees "compass sea and land to make one proselyte." The Pharisees were one of the principal groups that emerged under Hasmonean rule, an era to be discussed below. (The Sadducees and the Essenes were the two other major groups.) The Pharisees, the most significant of the three groups because it was through them that modern Judaism emerged, believed the idea that God spoke laws to Moses beyond the Torah and that these ideas were passed on. Additional Pharisee beliefs included the belief in an afterlife where there would be rewards and punishments and the eventual arrival of a Messiah. Clearly, Matthew's angry comment, however exaggerated, would not have resonance with the audience he wished to reach if proselytizing activities were not widely recognized.

The Roman writers who resented conversion activities have already been mentioned. Well-known writers such as Juvenal and Tacitus mocked those who sympathized with the Jews by celebrating the Sabbath and avoiding pork. These writers and others saw such sympathizers as traitors to Roman culture.

Additional evidence of Jewish proselytizing efforts can be seen in more dramatic fashion as well, especially in the expulsions from Rome because of their active efforts to encourage proselytes. There were at least two such expulsions. In fact, the first reference to Jews in Rome is in relation to their expulsion in 139 BCE, an expulsion explicitly caused by Jewish efforts to teach their religious rites to Romans. (It should be noted, once more, that some scholars read these efforts differently and do not see missionary activity as the cause of the expulsion).

The second expulsion of the Jews was in the year 19 CE and was done by the emperor Tiberius. At least one writer (Dio Cassius) connects this expulsion to Jewish missionary activity.

Given this evidence, it is time to consider the methods Jews used to undertake what they understood as their religious mission to proselytize.

One important method as Jews of the era understood it was to call on and count on God to intervene to bring about the conversion of the Gentiles. Sacred literature was filled with visions of the Gentiles coming to God. Tobit 13:11, for example, envisions Gentiles streaming to Zion. But this is at the end of time. It is a vision of redemption, not normal times. Perhaps 1 Enoch is the most inclusive writing about this vision.

Miracles performed by God can, in the sacred literature, lead to conversions before the end of time. For example, when Judith is saved, Achior embraces Judaism (Judith 11:23, 14:6–10). It was a theme in this literature that God's acts led Gentiles to convert, and not just at the moment when history ended.

The use of missionaries was another method to win adherents to Judaism. The term "missionary" is so tied in our language with the Christian understanding of the word that it is important to distinguish what is meant when we speak of someone as a "Jewish missionary." The idea of a Christian mission was much more urgent than that of any Jewish mission, at least for those who saw in Christianity the exclusive means of salvation. Judaism never claimed such exclusivity, so there was no sense that a person's soul was at stake in a conversion discussion. Christians greatly simplified the conversion process, so, for example, there was no requirement for circumcision. Christianity removed all the Jewish ritual requirements. No longer was work forbidden on the Sabbath. No longer was there a requirement to follow all the Jewish laws. Thus the job of a Christian missionary was, in some sense, much easier when dealing with pagans than the job of anyone who wished to convince the pagans to become Jewish.

Christians organized missionaries; Jews did not. It was, seemingly, Jewish individuals, not operating from some central organization, who encouraged converts.

All in all, it makes more sense to limit the word "missionary" to Christianity, to see it as perhaps rooted in Jewish efforts to win converts but with a new incentive (salvation), new requirements, and new methods.

What, then, should Jewish efforts be called? In general, it is more useful to consider Jewish efforts either literary, as discussed, or oral. These oral efforts might, for example, include readings, lectures, or private discussions. Jews were teachers, persuaders, not missionaries. They believed Judaism true and superior and said so, but they did not evidently believe that a person's fate after death depended on choosing Judaism. Their borderlines in engaging in persuasion were therefore almost by definition different from those of their Christian counterparts. Jewish preachers and teachers were among those who roamed the land.

So Jewish teachers instead of Jewish missionaries engaged in active efforts to win proselytes. There was no Jewish occupation devoted to proselytism. Instead, it was incumbent on every Jew to teach pagans the truth of Judaism. Therefore, the Jewish educators weren't at schools where pagans could go, but, as noted above, the teachers were often merchants who might discuss Judaism or answer questions about it when they were engaged in normal commercial activities. It is important to note that by this time, pagans were very interested in Judaism and often did ask such questions. Every Jew was, in theory at least, minimally learned about Jewish rituals and law. There were many Jewish refugees from Judea. Indeed, most of the proselytizing activities took place outside the Land of Israel, not in it. There were also, no doubt, professional lecturers who wanted through oral argument to convince their audience of the worth of Judaism. But they acted on individual impulse, not under communal command.

For example, there was an actor named Alityrus who was the person who interested Poppaea, Nero's wife, in becoming Jewish. Jews made personal approaches to people. These approaches might, for example, include an invitation to attend a synagogue, to participate in some Jewish ritual such as the celebration of a Sabbath meal, to hear an exposition of Jewish beliefs, or to read some of the available conversionary literature.

Because so many Jews were travelers, Gentiles came into frequent contact with them and saw their faithful practices, heard their prayers, were impressed by their business ethics, and so on. It was precisely because Jews educated everyone in the community, including children, that these merchants were often quite learned. Ordinary Jews, that is, were very capable of answering the questions they encountered and were reflexively and unconsciously often effective living models of what it meant to live as a Jew. It should be noted that Jews did not, for example, stop strangers on the street and preach to them. Jews considered this a pagan practice and so would not engage in it.

The Jewish repulsion at pagan practices extended to the widespread abandonment of children by pagan families. According to Philo, Jews frequently adopted these abandoned children and, in a way that might be considered conversionary, raised and educated them as Jews, including having them regularly attend synagogues.

The synagogue was a central institution in Jewish life, so it is unsurprising that it was a crucial institution in attracting converts. Philo ("De Septenario," 6) talks about thousands of houses of instructions in every town. Whether by invitation or personal curiosity, many Gentiles were drawn to the inner mysteries of the synagogue service. The synagogue served as the place where the Torah was read, discussed, analyzed, and interpreted. The very act of questioning, the variety of interpretations, the alluring stories of God and heroes, and the improbable majesty of Jewish history must all have been appealing to pagan observers hungry for meaning in their lives.

While it is possible to argue that, by definition, the exposition of Jewish sacred literature was a proselytizing activity, it is more precise to say that the synagogue service functioned incidentally to encourage conversions. That does not seem to have been its primary purpose. But, independent of its own intentions, the pageantry of the synagogue service and the alluring intellectual activity that was embedded in it did serve as an invitation to become part of the religious world the synagogue embodied.

The notion of incidental proselytizing is an important one. Jews didn't have to harangue, blackmail, or threaten. They used persuasion and modeling to make their case. Nowhere is this more obvious than in the Jewish enactment of moral behavior and good deeds. Without intending their moral impulses to encourage conversion to Judaism, the profound ethical foundation of Judaism, in theory and in practice, proved to be enormously appealing to Gentiles.

Romantic attachment was another incidental means of conversion. Jews, especially Jewish men, married women Gentiles who then frequently converted.

There was another means of conversion, less well known and far less savory. It was the use of force by the Hasmoneans.

The Hasmonean kingdom (110–63 BCE) was the focus of the next era of Jewish history. As more and more Jews became influenced by Greek culture, more conservative elements within Judaism became increasingly dissatisfied. After Alexander's death, Judea was an area subject to attack. In 198 BCE the Syrians gained control and concluded that the Hellenistic ways should be forced on the Jewish population. In reaction to this turmoil and seeking to suppress the Jewish dissatisfaction, in 169 BCE, the king Antiochus IV Epiphanes offered decrees that banned various Jewish religious rites. He forbade Sabbath worship and circumcision among those rites and then sent in troops to ensure that Greek ways were indeed followed. A Jewish priest named Mattathias and his five sons led a rebellion against the ruler. One son, Judah the Maccabee, became the leader of this effort. Judah recaptured the holy city of Jerusalem and cleansed the Temple of any pagan influences. The cleansing took eight days and forms the origin, along with the general triumph of foreign influences over Jewish rites, of the festival of Hanukkah.

The Hasmoneans succeeded the Maccabees as leaders of the people. The Hasmonean dynasty remained in power from 165 BCE to 63 BCE. A civil war led to the dissolution of the dynasty. The people, no longer wishing to be ruled by a king, appealed to the Romans, and the Romans eventually conquered the land.

But during the Hasmonean rule, conversion by force took place. John Hyrcanus, who reigned from 134 BCE to his death in 104 BCE, forcibly converted the Idumeans in 125 BCE. His son Artobulus I forced the Itureans to convert in 105 BCE. These forced conversions were evidently highly unusual in Jewish history, but there is some evidence that it was a policy during the Hasmonean rule. For example, according to Josephus (*Antiquities*, 13.397), Alexander Jannaeus (c. 80 BCE) destroyed the city of Pella in the land of Moab because those who lived there refused to adopt Jewish customs.

Who were those who converted during this era? There are individual proselytes beyond those already named. Here are just some of them:

Aquila, a translator of the Bible into Greek.
Avtalyon (Abtalion) was a Pharisee leader and rabbinic sage who lived in the middle of the first century BCE. He was the vice president of the Sanhedrin, or assembly, in Jerusalem.
Beturia Paulla, a Roman convert, embraced Judaism when she was seventy. She was called the "mother" of two synagogues, meaning she provided financial support. This fact provides at least anecdotal evidence that not all ancient proselytes were poor.
Bithiah was by tradition a pharaoh's daughter and an Egyptian princess who claimed Moses as her own son and brought

the infant into Pharaoh's house. Again according to tradition, she left Egypt, exiled for her actions, with Moses during the Exodus. She married Mered the Judahite and had three children.

Flavia Domitilla in Jewish tradition saved the Jews when the Roman emperor decreed that in a month's time the Senate would issue an order that all Jews and Christians in the Roman Empire be killed. Flavia convinced her husband, Flavius Clemens, to defend the Jewish people. Flavius himself was also supposed to have converted to Judaism after coming into contact with the great Jewish sage Rabbi Akiva.

Fulvia, the wife of Saturninus, who was a close friend of the emperor Tiberius, was convinced to convert to Judaism after she learned about the religion from a Jewish refugee who had come to Rome supposedly to avoid punishment. However, the man turned out to be a fraud. He and others convinced Fulvia to donate gold for the Temple in Jerusalem, but the conspirators kept all her contributions. By tradition, it was when Tiberius learned of the fraud from Saturninus that the emperor banned Jews from Rome in 19 CE.

Izates bar Monobaz, the king of Adiabene, an ancient kingdom in the land of Assyria, was a convert. Izates's mother, Queen Helena, who also converted, moved to Jerusalem, where she donated large amounts of money for the Temple and built palaces for herself and for both of her sons.

Makeda, the queen of Sheba.

Obadiah, a prophet.

Shmaya, a rabbi and sage who descended from King Sancheriv of Assyria, the man who destroyed the Kingdom of Israel. Shmaya led the Pharisees in the first century BCE and was president of the Sanhedrin.

Titus Flavius Clemens, the Roman emperor Vespasian's great-
nephew.

Yael, whose story of saving Israel is told in the Book of Judges.

There were other converts in ancient times as well, and they will
be discussed in later chapters.

There was, according to some scholars, another category of
people during the Hellenistic and Roman periods who were not
Gentiles but also were not full converts. These people were
known as "God-fearers" or "sympathizers." These semiproselytes
may, in fact, have really also been proselytes but with a different
name. But it is precisely because Jews were so successful in attracting and absorbing converts during this era that it makes logical sense that there existed a group that was between the two, not
pagan but not yet fully Jewish. There was a later distinction made
in the Talmud between the groups. A *ger tsedek* was a proselyte
who was a full convert, who accepted all the responsibilities of
Jewish life, who promised to observe all the laws of the Torah. In
contrast, the *ger toshav* had given up the idolatry of paganism but
had not yet decided to accept the laws and ritual obligations of
the Jews. It is widely believed that early Christianity found a
receptive audience among the latter group, for they were attracted to some of the ideas of Judaism but not desirous of following all its laws. Christianity provided them with a belief in a God,
including in Jesus a God they could see, whereas Judaism's God
was wholly indivisible and invisible.

What ceremonies were required for full conversion during this
time? The three, by consensus of scholars, include circumcision, a
water purification (later in Jewish life a *mikveh* and the antece-
dent of the Christian rite of baptism), and a sacrifice. The limitations of this consensus, however, lie in a contradiction. By most
evidence, there were more female converts to Judaism than male
converts, yet the written records were about the requirements for
a male convert. It may be that, like Ruth, a female convert simply

had to make a declaration of allegiance or may also have been required, as now, to do a water purification rite. It may also be that the "requirement" of a sacrifice in the Temple is inaccurate, that the conversion led rather to the right to offer such a sacrifice. There is other evidence (as we shall see in the next chapter in a story about Hillel converting a pagan) that even the requirement of circumcision was not always demanded.

The reasonable conclusion is that it is probable that circumcision was required for males, that water purification may have been, and that some converts gave sacrifices. It seems most probable that new converts had to abandon pagan beliefs and believe in and worship the one God, that they had to study the Torah, pray, follow such laws as existed, and in general absorb the Jewish way of life, including its ethical temperament.

The Second Temple period was not going to last. History never seemed to leave the Jews alone.

After the Roman general Pompey conquered the land and destroyed the Hasmonean dynasty in 63 BCE, Judea came under Roman occupation and control. The Senate in Rome appointed Herod the Great to be the king of Judea. The Romans were often openly hostile to Jews, and this led to a Jewish revolt in 66 CE. Finally, in the year 70 CE., the Second Temple was destroyed by the Romans (on Tisha B'Av, the same day of the Jewish year as the First Temple had been destroyed; the date, marking other tragedies as well, is remembered each year by fasting and prayer). Jews continued living in Judea, and eventually there was another revolt in 132–136 CE known as the Bar Kokhba revolt. The devastating loss of Jewish lives led to a thorough reorganization of Jewish life, since so many Jews now lived outside of the Land of Israel, dispersed and living in what became known as the Diaspora, that is, any land outside the Promised Land. The Jews had to figure out a new way to survive, to come up with laws to govern a life again without their nation.

3

A FENCE AROUND THE TORAH

Converts in the Talmudic Era

As the Romans were attacking Jerusalem and destroying the Second Temple, the Jews, especially in the Diaspora, were struggling to redefine Jewish life. There was to be no more Temple at which to offer sacrifices. No more priests. No more sacred homeland. As had happened with the dispersal to Babylonia, the Jewish people faced the real possibility of extinction.

But in this case, there was no Cyrus to conquer Babylon and send the Jews home—that is, to seize control of the land from Rome and allow the Jews to rebuild their Temple.

Before the Temple's destruction but predicting it, Yohnanan ben Zakkai, a rabbi, escaped the Roman siege of Jerusalem during the fighting by hiding in a coffin and approached Vespasian, then a Roman general, with a request. Ben Zakkai wanted to start a small academy at Yavneh. It had a simple purpose: teach the Bible to Jewish children.

Once the Temple was destroyed, the academy became functionally the reestablished Sanhedrin, the religious center of Jewish life from which scholars could decide how to reconstruct Jewish life. The rabbis there had an incredible and overwhelming task. All the principal institutions of Jewish life were destroyed. How could Judaism continue?

The academy replaced the Temple. Rabbis replaced the priests. Study and prayer replaced the sacrifices. The rabbis began studying, talking, and writing down their thoughts. They conceived of what they were doing as the oral Torah, the companion to the written Torah given to Moses at Mount Sinai. A tradition developed that God had also given the oral Torah and it had been passed down generation to generation until the rabbis wrote it down finally.

The era from the first through the fifth century—that is, prior to what is often called the Middle Ages—may for the sake of proselytism be called the Talmudic era. It was the time the Talmud was compiled, and in Roman it was a time of transition from pagan emperors to Christian ones and a time of the consolidation of Christian dominance and power.

The Jews focused on their own survival. By the year 200 CE, the oral law had been collected in the Mishnah. Jewish power continued to dissolve. The Roman Empire was crumbling from within, and a new religion, Christianity, was continuing to grow. That growth was exemplified by the crucial conversion of the emperor Constantine in 313 CE. Anti-Jewish legislation ensued. The Jews were powerless, without a homeland or Temple, increasingly the object of religious hatred, and demoralized. Unsurprisingly, the Jews increasingly turned inward, focusing on study and religious observance.

There were Jews throughout the Diaspora. Especially active Jewish scholars, for example, lived in Babylonia. They also established academies and studied the Mishnah, commenting on it. Their work, called the Gemara, combined with the Mishnah to form the Babylonian Talmud. (There was also a Gemara produced in Jerusalem, but it is briefer and less frequently used). Once the Talmud was completed, it was the various heads of the

Jewish academies who ruled Jewish life. Each head was called a *gaon*, and the years 600–1000 CE are frequently referred to as the gaonic age.

This rapid decline of Jewish fortune after the Roman defeat of Jewish rebellions marked an end to the great era of Jewish proselytism. After all, Jews were focused on survival, on developing institutions to replace the major ones that had been destroyed. They were dispirited. They were probably filled with doubts about their future. They turned inward, not outward toward attracting others. Rabbis in the Talmud wrote about building "a fence around the Torah" and in so doing keeping Jews within the fence and outsiders away. It was an attempt at intellectual isolation in the name of regrouping and survival.

This inward turning was complemented by the Roman and increasingly Christian hostility. The Romans made it punishable by death for Jews to seek converts or people to embrace Judaism. For example, converts were persecuted by Domitian between 81 and 96 CE. Any property the converts had was confiscated. Sometimes instead of a death sentence they were sent into exile. In 131 CE Hadrian prohibited any public instruction in Jewish subjects and any circumcisions. Five years later, he added that the Sabbath could not be observed and no Jewish ritual could be performed in public. In the year 200 (from now on all years will be in the Common Era), the emperor Septimius Severus forbade heathens to embrace Judaism. In 325, not long after he became a Christian, Constantine reenacted Hadrian's law making it illegal for Jews to convert slaves or engage in any activity that would encourage people to convert to Judaism. In 330, the emperor Constantius decreed that if the Jews had converted slaves, those slaves would be forfeited and if any Christian slave had been circumcised, the Jews who ordered the rite would be executed and their property seized.

These laws were not the only reason proselytism slowed. Christianity offered its own version of a belief in one God without all of Judaism's ritual requirements, without the obligation, for example, to keep the Sabbath or eat only restricted foods. Christianity required faith in Jesus, not in Jewish laws. Many people who might have embraced Judaism chose the Christian path instead.

It might at this point be useful to define more precisely the differences between Judaism and Christianity on some key issues. It should be noted, of course, that because Christianity emerged from Judaism there are similarities as well, so it is somewhat misleading to focus only on the differences. But it was those differences that created friction between the two religions, resulting in a major change in Jewish history. Indeed, however comforting the thought, it is misleading to think of the two religions as essentially the same, as some converts tried to do, or even to see Christianity as a natural evolution of Judaism. The two have separate worldviews with distinctly different beliefs as well as practices. While there certainly was hostility between the two religions, from Judaism's point of view, all people are the children of one God. All people receive help and love from God. Having said that, let us focus on some differences between Judaism and Christianity.

Those differences start with different conceptions of God. Judaism's central idea is its insistence on a pure form of monotheism, the idea that there is one unified God. Therefore, according to Judaism, God cannot be made up of parts, even if, in theory, those parts are thought to be united. So Christianity's foundational idea of a Trinity, that God is made up of God the Father, God the Son (Jesus), and God the Holy Spirit, is not acceptable to Jews.

For Christians, Jesus is the central figure of their religion, the Son of God, the one who saves souls, who is the Messiah, the man who was also God and God's revelation in the flesh. Jesus absorbs human sins and therefore frees from sins those who accept his divinity. The Jewish view of Jesus is much different. Since for Jews God can't be human, Jesus can't be seen as the Son of God or the Messiah. However great a teacher and parable creator Jesus may have been, finally, for Jews, he was just a compelling human figure, a Son of God only in the metaphorical sense that all humans are children of God. For Jews, Jesus is not the being who saves souls.

Other differences between the religions are more hazy because of the wide variety of differences within the religions themselves. Consider, for example, the subjects of free will and original sin. Jewish thought does not admit the idea of humans being born with original sin, that they are evil at birth and incapable of removing that stain by themselves but rather need the act of grace provided by a belief in Jesus, whose death atoned for human sins. Jews, in general, believe that humans are born neither naturally good nor naturally evil but rather have a good and bad inclination built into them. They have the free moral will to make a choice between the good and the bad—that is, in theory, the good can overcome any evil inclination.

There is an emphasis in much of mainstream Christianity on death, on heaven, and, at least at key times in human history, on hell as well. Jewish thought tends to focus on the life lived on earth and maximizing its worth. There are vivid descriptions of the afterlife in both religions, though they are more well-known in Christianity. Jewish descriptions were mainly done in the Middle Ages and never became widely taught in contemporary Jewish life. There was a Jewish belief in an afterlife where justice would prevail, where humans would be at a greater or lesser distance from God, depending on the moral lives they led. But views of the afterlife are individual choices for Jews rather than mandated teachings.

There are many other differences, but these are the key ones. Because Jews, for example, did not believe salvation required becoming Jewish, whereas Christians believed salvation required a belief in Jesus, Christianity transformed the Jewish concept of conversion from an ideal, a devout wish, a divine expectation, into a religious requirement for salvation and transformed the means of effecting conversion from, most typically, literature and oral persuasion to widespread missionary work.

The Jewish mission itself had been altered from seeing Judaism as a religion to be offered to all who wished to learn it to seeing Judaism as endangered and needing to be saved. The Jews focused on their religion, on the obligation of ritual observance rather than the prior focus on national self-defense and militarism as a means of survival. The rabbis (the word means "teacher") saw themselves as educators, making sure the surviving Jews and the next generation carried their Judaism wherever they might go. A conqueror might take away land and property but could not take away learning. Just as God was portable, able to be worshipped in any land, so was Judaism, able to be studied wherever Jews were in the world. Portability became a crucial means for survival. The rabbinic mission was precisely that survival. First they had to save themselves and their people before they saved humanity.

The rabbis were in a sense trapped when it came to proselytism. They could praise it, including praising it in their daily prayer book. But they were legitimately fearful of persecution. The Jews were segregating from Gentiles, forced by persecution and hatred and internally driven by trauma and the need to focus on learning and prayer.

All of this combined for a steep declination in Jewish conversionary activities. Jews still passively welcomed converts, but widespread efforts ceased or remained hidden. If encouraging converts could (and did) endanger the very fragile existence of the surviving Jewish community, the Jews and their rabbinical leaders took the most prudential approach they could and severely limited their conversionary activities.

It should be noted that the very existence of the anticonversionary laws is an indication that they were needed, that Romans wanted to convert and that Jews continued to seek converts. And it should also be considered that by pausing in their conversionary activity and regrouping, the rabbis were in a sense preserving the Jewish people for the day when their proselytizing mission could be renewed. As history turned out, of course, this hesitation to seek converts turned into the norm. Jews began falsely to see not accepting converts as the normative Jewish tradition. That is not to say there were no supporters of conversion. In the fourth century, the Babylonian scholars Raba and Rab Ashi were vocal in their support of proselytism. Evidently, entire villages approached Rabbah ben Aboah to seek conversion. The Talmud notes that Mahoza, a major Jewish community, had many converts to Judaism (Avodah Zarah 64a; Kiddushin 73a).

Part of the Jewish attitude during these trying times can be discerned by what the rabbis wrote in the Talmud. It is misleading to think of all the Talmudic literature as one book. The different writings were developed over a long period of time in different places. It makes more sense to examine the statements in the chronological order in which they were written. In his book *The Stranger within Your Gates: Converts and Conversion in Rabbinic Literature*, Gary G. Porton does exactly that. Here, a sample of rabbinic comments will be considered. Porton's research is important, for example, in showing that it took much longer than previously thought for the rabbis to develop a standard conversion ceremony.

The most famous of all the stories about a convert to Judaism in the Talmud involves two competing rabbis. Hillel, the head of the Sanhedrin from 30 BCE to 10 CE, famously admired converts. As he reportedly said (Pirke Avot 1:12): "Be of the disciples of Aaron, loving peace and pursuing peace, loving other people and drawing them near to the Torah." This passage seems to refer to proselytizing efforts.

There were a variety of conversionary stories involving Hillel (Shabbat 31a). In one story, a pagan wished to be converted but only if he could be allowed to observe solely the written law, the Torah, and not the oral law embodied in the Talmud. Hillel's colleague Shammai refused such a request from someone who clearly wished to accept only part of the Jewish religion. Hillel, though, took another approach. First, Hillel taught the Hebrew alphabet to the pagan. On the next day, though, Hillel reversed the order of the letters in the alphabet. This reversal naturally annoyed the would-be convert. Hillel said that even the order of the Hebrew alphabet was dependent on the oral law. The religion, Hillel said, made no sense without studying it in the right order, which required mastery of the oral law.

The single most famous of the stories involving Hillel is this one. A pagan approached the great scholar Shammai and sought to have some fun at the rabbi's expense. The pagan, in a way that was mocking, said to Shammai, "I am willing to convert to Judaism but only on the condition that you teach me the whole of the Torah while I stand on one foot." Shammai grew angry and chased the pagan away with a builder's tool. The pagan then approached Rabbi Hillel with the same statement. But Hillel did not chase him away. Instead, even while knowing the pagan was making fun of him, Hillel said: "What is hateful to you do not do to your neighbor. That is the whole Torah. The rest is commentary. Go and study it."

The rabbis accepted Hillel's teaching rather than Shammai's. Hillel's was an interesting approach. He accepted a convert before the convert studied. He was willing to accept a convert who had no clearly good motive. Hillel, then, must have seen encouraging converts as so important a religious imperative that he sought to be as friendly and as welcoming as he could possibly be, even in the face of mockery.

There is another interesting aspect to the tale. Hillel's injunction is frequently compared to the Golden Rule: Do unto others as you would have others do unto you. But, the argument goes, Hillel simply put that rule in a negative form. Hillel's construction, however, is more morally subtle. Consider a masochist, for example, a person who derives pleasure from receiving pain. If the masochist followed the Golden Rule literally, the masochist would inflict pain on others for the masochist enjoys receiving the pain. But in Hillel's construction, the masochist has no moral room to inflict pain.

A third story was about a potential convert who would become Jewish if he could receive a promise that he would become the high priest. (This event took place, of course, before the Romans defeated the Jews, destroyed the Temple, and ended the priesthood.) Shammai turned him away, but Hillel accepted him as a student and showed him that even King David would not qualify because the priesthood was hereditary.

There were specific converts mentioned throughout Talmudic literature, although in many cases we simply have names, but the specific listing is one more sign of rabbinical acceptance. Some of those converts not mentioned elsewhere in this chapter include: the Nablatah family, Abba Saul ben Batnit, Judah the Ammonite, Ketiah ben Shalom, Johanan ben Torta, Neophytos, Rabbi Judah ben Gerim, Rabbi Judah Nesiah, the Ashtor family, Rabbi Samuel bar Shilath, Rabbi Samuel bar Judah, Rabbi Isaac ben Jacob, and Rabbi Judah the Hindu. It might seem surprising that so many of those mentioned went from convert to rabbi. But history was often written about the elites, and Talmudic writers would have been proud that many famous rabbis were converts or descendants of converts.

There were many other important statements about conversion in the Talmudic era. The post-Mishnaic tractate *gerim* offered a procedure by which converts could be welcomed, offered regulations to cover circumcisions, ritual baths, and sacrifices, defined the *ger toshav*, and served to remind Jews that they had to continue having a warm and welcoming attitude toward potential converts. This manual of conversionary laws is an interesting indication that there continued to be in Jewish life an impulse to continue their perceived obligation to proselytize.

There are a variety of comments in Talmudic literature about conversion. Some of the comments are negative, but most are positive. Given the persecution the Jews faced from Rome, the competition from Christianity, and the trauma of their loss of nation and Temple, it is amazing that encouraging converts was considered at all.

The most famous of the many positive comments in the Talmud about conversion was made by Rabbi Johanan and agreed with by Rabbi Eleazar (Pesachim 87b) in an astonishing assertion that God's purpose in exiling the Jews from their sacred homeland was for only one reason, and that was to increase the number of converts. It is particularly striking that so horrific an event as the loss of national sovereignty and the destruction of central religious institutions could justifiably be seen as having a divine purpose. That purpose of seeking converts had to have been seen by Rabbi Johanan as of such overwhelming importance to God that it justified trauma and exile. In what might be seen as a companion passage (Nedarim 32a), Rabbi Johanan declares that Abraham had been punished and his descendants had to suffer slavery in Egypt because "he prevented people from entering under the wings of the Shekhinah."

In Jewish religious literature, converts frequently are cast as being as beloved and close to God as are born Jews. "Dear are converts, for in every place the Torah warns against [abusing] them" (Mekhilta Nezlkin 18 on 22:20). Jeremiah 14:8 notes: "Our Rabbis say: Dear is the convert, for the Holy One had written of Himself." And "'Why shouldest Thou be as a stranger in the land?' said the Holy One: Thus do I cherish the convert. And Abraham was a convert" (Lech Leka, 6).

Some commentators even assert that God is closer to converts than to born Jews. Resh Lakish (in Lech Leka 6) noted, "The proselyte who converts is dearer than Israel were when they stood before Mount Sinai. Why? Because had they not seen the thunders and the lightning and the mountains quaking and the sound of the horns, they would not have accepted the Torah. But this one, who saw none of these things, came, surrendered himself to the Holy One, and accepted upon himself the Kingdom of Heaven. Could any be dearer than he?"

Other positive references include those by Rabbi Abbahu, who interpreted various biblical passages as encouraging proselytism.

What may be understood as evidence that there were widespread conversions can be seen in Shir ha-Shirim Rabbah, a commentary on the Song of Solomon. There it is written: "As the old man sat preaching, many proselytes were converting at that time." This conclusion is buttressed by the commentary on Ecclesiastes: "All the rivers run into the sea, yet the sea is not full. All the proselytes enter Israel, yet Israel is not diminished."

An interesting parable is in Numbers Rabbah 8:2 showing God's love of converts. Additional references praising converts can be found in such places as Hagigah 5a, 8 and Genesis Rabbah 34:14.

There are several negative comments about converts in the Talmud as well. The most famous of these is by Rabbi Helbo (Yevamot 109b), who asserts that converts are as troublesome as a sore or scab. But, as has been done, even this comment can be interpreted in different ways. It is possible, for example, that Rabbi Helbo was making a straightforward historical observation, that since Roman and Christian authorities meted out punishment to both the convert and the Jewish community when a conversion took place, converts unintentionally were a source of trouble in the sense of being politically dangerous but may simultaneously have been a source of pride. The great scholar Maimonides, though, believed the negative comment was limited in scope, referring only to those who converted with an ulterior motive, and that the comment did not include the overwhelming number of people who genuinely converted for good reasons (Mishneh Torah V, I chapter 13, no. 8). Other commentators had an extraordinarily supportive interpretation: that converts were so careful about keeping all the commandments that they made it difficult for born Jews who, in comparison, did not wish to be seen as being lax about obeying divine law. However, even if we take Rabbi Helbo's words as simple and direct in their hostility, they were uttered by an individual and do not represent the typical thinking of the rabbis.

However, there were other negative comments. Rabbi Helbo, for example, thought that proselytes delayed the arrival of the Messiah (Niddah 12b). Rabbi Isaac bar Joseph believed that "one evil thing after another befalls those who accept proselytes."

But these hostile comments are a sociological milestone. First, they illustrate that conversions to Judaism continued despite the legal restrictions, the punishments, the competition from Christianity, and so on. And the passages also indicate that there was a great deal of internal discussion about welcoming converts. The negative comments are precisely important because they are indicative of a turn in Jewish attitude, a sense that welcoming converts was not, indeed, part of the Jewish mission but rather a burden to the Jewish community and so an effort that should be avoided. It was this attitude that, over the centuries, hardened into folk wisdom so that even today many born Jews see conversion as an un-Jewish activity and sometimes question whether converts can ever be genuinely members of the Jewish tribe.

Beyond Talmudic literature, the era's interest in proselytism can also be seen in a variety of other ways, such as Roman legislation.

The legislation that the Romans made against proselytism is mostly seen in terms of religious intolerance. That, however, is anachronistic, for the pagans' religion of Rome was not in competition for religious superiority with Judaism. Rather, when a pagan became Jewish, Rome was concerned that the pagan's national interests changed, that the conquered, rebellious Judea would have another supporter, and that the conquering Roman Empire would have one fewer supporter. Thus the conversionary legislation can most accurately be seen as a political act, a punishment for the past rebellion and an attempt to forestall any future rebellions by limiting fighters and political supporters. The Jews, after all, had rebelled during the years 66–74, 115–117, and 132–135. Additionally, even if the new Jews might not have supported rebels within Judea, the Romans still had to fight barbarians and their fierce enemies, the Parthians. The Romans were concerned that a larger Jewish population in the Parthian Empire would foment rebellion and fighting just as they had done in Judea.

It is not the case that the Roman fears were without foundation. For in the year 351, the Jews did again rebel, mostly because of persecution by Christians. Under their leader Patricius, the Jews fought against an overwhelming enemy.

Most of the legislation the Romans promulgated focused on Jewish practices. The first explicit ban on proselytism, however, came about in 198–199, when the emperor Septimius Severus visited Judea and, without apparent explanation, made becoming Jewish a forbidden act. This ban, however, was ineffective. We can see this because there are records of several converts. For example, a man named Domnus converted to Judaism from

Christianity when the Christians were persecuted in Egypt at the start of the third century. This fact indicates that even with the legislation, it evidently was more dangerous to convert to Christianity than it was to convert to Judaism.

There were sixty-six laws pertaining to Jews contained in the *Codex Theodosianus* (*Book of Theodosianus*), a work compiling the laws of the Roman Empire under Christian emperors, beginning in 312. A commission to compile those laws was established by Theodosius II in 429, and the compilation was finally published in 438. Of those sixty-six Jewish-related laws, fourteen of them, more than one-fifth, dealt with the proselytism of people who were free, and twelve of them dealt with converting slaves. Two had to do with God-fearers. Clearly, the emperors saw proselytism as a threat against their state. The dates of the laws are also interesting. Two are from the third century, nine are from the fourth century, fourteen are from the fifth century, and three are from the sixth century. It should also be noted that even this compilation does not include all the laws made by emperors.

Beyond Jewish literature and Roman legislation, the story of conversion to Judaism can also be determined by various church canons. During the Christian church's early years of success and attempt to consolidate its power, especially, that is, during the third and fourth centuries, Judaism posed a variety of threats. Some Christians, for example, citing the fact that Christianity had absorbed the Hebrew Bible as its own though naming it the "Old Testament" thought that it was then logical to adopt Jewish ritual laws. Of that group, some continued on the same logical path and became fully Jewish. Other Christians were attracted to Judaism because they saw it as the people and religion into which Jesus had chosen to be born. Jews were also accused of supporting or at least supplementing the various Christian heresies that arose. The church, that is, grew increasingly hostile as its power grew.

But that hostility emerged early in church history. In 52, there was a synod in Jerusalem to deal with, among other questions, how the church should deal with Jews. Later synods were concerned with such questions as intermarriage because so many Christian women who married Jews ended up converting to Judaism. There were many references to Jewish proselytism in Christian literature. To take just one example, in the fourth century, Ephraem Syrus noted, probably using expansive and exaggerated prose, that many heathens were fooled into converting by Jewish missionaries. Even if this is exaggerated, however, the reference is important for two reasons. First, it illustrates that proselytism continued throughout the Talmudic era and during the rise of Christianity. Second, it adds to the great mystery of proselytism. There are so many references to it, so many examples in the literature, in Roman legislation, and in Christian writing that it remains a puzzle that there is not a record of the name of any person with the specific and exclusive job of Jewish missionary. It may be, of course, that there was no job. It may also be that, for very different reasons, rabbinic and Christian leaders of the time wished to suppress records of such people. It may be that Jewish missionaries didn't want to have their names recorded because they faced internal opposition from rabbis worried about any possible punishments meted out to Jews by authorities for proselytizing efforts and because they faced external opposition from those authorities.

Of all the church fathers, it is John Chrysostom (c. 347–407), the bishop of Antioch, who is the most vehemently and articulately bitter about Jewish efforts to win converts. His dates are odd in a way. After all, it was in 324 that Judea, now mockingly renamed Palestine by the Romans because they wanted to replace the Jewish name Israel with a word derived from the name of the Israelites' ancient enemies, the Philistines, became a Christian protectorate. Many Jews there became Christians. Additionally, it was in

380 when the emperor Theodosius I declared Orthodox Christianity as the empire's religion. It should have been seen as the triumph of Christianity over Judaism. There was, it might be concluded, no reason to keep attacking Jews. They had lost. And yet it was six years later that Chrysostom delivered sermons against those he called "Judaizers." Christians, especially Christian women, were attracted to Judaism.

There is an irony to Chrysostom's complaints. He doesn't see the problem emerging from Jewish proselytism but from Christians who alerted other Christians to the attractions of Judaism. It was the emphasis, that is, on Christian mission that unintentionally sometimes found form in missionizing on behalf of Judaism.

It still took half a century, but it is safe to approximate that by 425 or 450 the Christian state was established, able to suppress heresies and generally in control enough to say that the era of any widespread proselytism was over. Since the time of Alexander, the Jews had been exceedingly open to and, depending on the definition, welcoming or actively encouraging and seeking converts. The Jewish attitude was one of mission, that it was a Jewish obligation to draw converts nearer to God and the Torah.

But the traumas of Jewish history had many effects. One of them was that the Jewish attitude toward proselytism changed. Consider the situation through the lens of a modern term. The Stockholm syndrome is a psychological state in which those held hostage express sympathy and sometimes empathy toward those who hold them captive. The Jews were psychological captives. The Christians actively and aggressively opposed Jewish proselytism. To protect themselves physically, the Jews, consciously or not, changed their psychological attitudes toward conversion. They came to oppose it, to see it, ironically, as a paradigmatically Christian, not a Jewish, activity. The Jews took on the psychological state of their religious competitors and, increasingly, persecutors.

In some sense, much like the history of Jewish nationalism, it may be the case that history skips centuries, going from ancient times to the modern era. But history is more subtle than that. It is not the case, for example, that Jews ever completely abandoned their nation. Jews continued to live and work and pray there across the centuries until their impulse for national identity re-emerged most strongly at the end of the nineteenth century. So, too, with proselytism. It may be that a conversion to Judaism might usefully end in the year 425 and then continue at some point in the twentieth century. But such a view misses what is almost a secret history. For during the Middle Ages and early modern times, Jews, often quietly, welcomed converts and con-tinued to have internal debates. While the conversions were rela-tively few in number, their very existence is a tribute to the power of the vital idea of proselytism. And there were, as we shall see, continuing dramatic instances of conversion.

Ironically, the continuing attractions of Judaism for converts are startling precisely because they came at a time when the Jew-ish nation had been conquered, when the Second Temple had been razed, when legislation against proselytism grew, when Christianity emerged first as a simple outgrowth and competitor of Judaism and then as a triumphant competitor. The lure of Judaism provides ongoing proof to the insights, beauty, and value of it as a religion and of its adherents as a people.

The Jews were going to have centuries in which they had to endure. Through it all they had the religion that so many found so attractive. Ironically, Jews, turning inward, were increasingly re-luctant to share that attractive religion even if there were Gentiles who continued to want to join the Jewish people.

4

THE TIME OF RELIGIOUS STRUGGLE

Converts in the Medieval Era

There was a dramatic story of conversion to Judaism in the Middle Ages, the embrace of Judaism by the Khazars. But the active encouragement of converts receded, and the widespread attachment to the Jewish people slowed to a small number of hardy souls. That is not to say that the vision of a moment in time when all peoples would embrace what the Jews deeply believed was the one true God disappeared. It was too deeply embedded within the Jewish belief system and Jewish liturgy for that to happen. But the end of days, like the revival of a Jewish nation, was to be left to God, not to human agency. There were justified prudential concerns about Jewish safety if the Jews did any proselytizing. Conversion as an act became increasingly identified with active Christian efforts to convince and then force Jews to abandon their religion. This made conversion as an act seem repulsive. And while Christians felt a need to convert souls because a foundational Christian belief was that there was no salvation outside the church, Jews had no such similar need. Jews didn't believe people had to be Jewish in order to enter heaven. The righteous of all nations had a place in the world to come. Absent this powerful impulse, the Jews didn't have the sort of missionary zeal that

Christians had. All this made conversions not just reduced in number but slowly erased from Jewish communal concerns and sense of missionary obligation. Conversion, once seen as a religious obligation, was no longer seen that way.

Yet, however dormant, the idea of conversion remained. The concept was transformed from acts of active encouragement to passive acceptance. The Jews didn't seek converts, but their exemplary religious behavior was supposed to be so attractive that some Gentiles would want to attach themselves to the Jewish people. For those Jews who saw Diaspora life as God's design to bring such a religious example to humanity, the idea of mission continued. Examples of such behavior can be found in the Talmud.

For example, Simeon ben Shetach was a poor man who nonetheless always acted ethically in all business matters involving the linen goods he bought and sold. One of his pupils, seeking to please him, went to a Gentile merchant and purchased a donkey. The Talmudic law about such purchases was that once the donkey was purchased, all that was on it also belonged to the new owner. Simeon gratefully accepted the gift, took off the saddle, and underneath it found an expensive jewel. Simeon's students were overjoyed because their master was now a wealthy man. After all, the jewel was on the donkey and all on the donkey legally belonged to Simeon. But Simeon knew that the merchant had not intended to sell the jewel, and so Simeon returned the jewel to the merchant, who exclaimed, "Blessed be the Lord, the God of Simeon ben Shetach" (Yerushalmi Bava Metzia, ii, 8c).

The rise of Islam greatly affected Jews in the Middle Ages. Jews in Arabia, Mesopotamia, and Persia were under the rule of yet another religious movement that believed it had replaced Judaism. The effect of Islam's swift surge in history had another effect as well. Potential converts to Judaism had a choice between a triumphant Christianity with increasing power, the new Islamic faith, or the poor, downtrodden, persecuted Jews, who had lost their homeland and Temple. It is easy to imagine a potential convert concluding a lesson from history that God had abandoned the Jews and favored Christianity or Islam.

And, in case such conclusions were not drawn, legal prohibitions continued. Between 395 and 408, Arcadius, the Byzantine emperor, reenacted Constantius's decrees that prohibited Jewish proselytizing. In 538 and 548, the Third and Fourth Councils of Orléans prohibited Jews from proselytizing. Between 717 and 720, Omar II prohibited Jews from seeking converts from among the Muslim population. In 740, Egbert, the Archbishop of York, in England, prohibited Christians from attending any Jewish religious festivals.

In the fourth century there was a synod in Laodicea in Asia Minor that prohibited widespread social contacts between Jews and Christians precisely to protect Christians from outside religious influence. The Council of Chalcedon, which took place in 451, made it illegal for Christians to marry Jews. The Trullan Synod of 692 included a resolution that Christians could not eat matzoh, or be friendly with Jews, or accept medicine from them, or bathe with them.

The situation worsened in the seventh century. Any Jews who were responsible for a Christian converting to Judaism would be subject to the death penalty and have all their goods seized.

By 1233 Pope Gregory IX ordered all copies of the Talmud to be seized and asked all German clerics to confront Christians who wished to embrace Judaism. In France, the Inquisition burned Rabbi Isaac Males of Toulouse because he had been responsible for Gentiles converting to Judaism.

Understandably, many conversions that did occur took place in areas attached to but not part of the lands where Christians or Muslims ruled. One way of interpreting this geographical fact is that Jews were engaging in political resistance of a sort, seeking to resist the encroaching power of both daughter religions.

Besides the Khazars, who will be discussed below, the most famous conversion was that of Yusuf Dhu Nuwas, the king of Himyar, in what is now Yemen. Dhu Nuwas (the name means "curly locks" and was in fact his nickname) was the ruler from 520 to 525. He made Judaism the state religion. While in power, he sought to convert nearby tribes to Judaism by force. Ethiopian Christians were, of course, violently opposed to such efforts and sent their army to stop such missionary efforts. Dhu Nuwas was defeated in battle and committed suicide by riding his horse over a cliff and into the sea.

There were, perhaps surprisingly, still a relatively large number of individual converts during the Middle Ages. The attractions of such a religion might seem elusive. But Judaism was seen by some as exotic and by others as even occult, having some kind of magical power. Christians were still often uncertain about their theology. Jews, in fact, were often forced into debates defending their presumably inferior religion. But Jews were often learned scholars who impressed the crowds. Judaism had the air of the forbidden, the secret. It was, for some, still the faith that Jesus had chosen to be born into and live his life. That was good enough for them. The Hebrew Bible, part of the Christian Bible, was read, and the Jewish kings, prophets, and heroes became part of ordinary people's consciousness.

It should also be mentioned that those who kept the chronicles of Jewish life were carefully supervised by Christian censors. They would therefore be very careful about mentioning any converts for fear of being responsible for the death or punishment of the convert and negative repercussions for the Jewish community. Therefore, there may have been many more conversions than we know about.

Another rarely mentioned point is that slaves were one of the sources of converts in the Middle Ages. Their story is an unusual one resulting originally from differing rules about slaves among Jews and Christians. According to the Torah, Hebrews had to release Hebrew slaves after seven years. Paul in the New Testament was understood to believe that Christians were not under any such obligation to free slaves. So slaves understandably desired to be a slave to Jews because then they would be free in seven years. Enough slaves became Jewish because of this that Jews were eventually not allowed to hold any slaves at all.

Despite all the limitations on Jews, there are a number of cases of individual conversions that have been passed on through Jewish history.

Some of the most noted conversions involved Christian clergy who became Jewish. Probably because of the sheer unlikeliness of such conversions and their obvious controversy and potential for friction, the very notoriety of such converts ensured their place in history.

For example, at the start of the seventh century, there was a monk who lived in the monastery on Mount Sinai. Whatever it was that drew him to Judaism, he decided that he should change his faith. Perhaps it was a vision that finally convinced him. In that vision, which he had as he was doing penance, he saw Jesus, the apostles, and Christian martyrs standing in a thick darkness, and Moses, the prophets, and the Israelites standing on the other side bathed in light. The monk crossed the desert and made his way to Tiberias. There he took the name of Abraham, a common practice, married, and had children.

Or consider the case of the Carolingian bishop Bodo (c. 814–876), who was a palace deacon to Emperor Louis the Pious. Bodo decided to go on a pilgrimage to Rome in 838. Whatever happened on that journey, a year later Bodo converted to Judaism, adopted the Jewish name Eleazar, and married the daughter of a Jewish friend. He fled to Saragossa in Spain and there incited the Moorish government to persecute Christians. He attempted to convert Christians to Judaism and wrote materials critical of Christianity. In 840, Eleazar began corresponding with Pablo Alvaro of Cordova, another part of Spain controlled by the Muslims. There was an interesting irony to the correspondence because Alvaro had been born Jewish but eventually converted to Christianity. They each wanted the other to return to the religions of their birth. Some of this correspondence is still available.

Wecelin was a cleric who worked for Duke Conrad of Carinthia (a nephew of Emperor Conrad II). In the early eleventh century, around 1005, Wecelin converted to Judaism and wrote a missionary pamphlet aimed at Christians, seeking their conversion. Part of that pamphlet still exists.

Other eleventh-century converts included Andreas, an archbishop of Bari, who became Jewish in about 1070.

There is a variety of anonymous converts. The most famous of the others is Obadiah, who was born in Oppido, Italy, late in the eleventh century. Obadiah named Andreas as inspiring him to convert, but Obadiah also had some sort of mystical dream. Evidently, Obadiah came to Jerusalem in 1096 along with soldiers during the First Crusade. He became Jewish in 1102.

There was another famous convert named Obadiah who was probably born a Muslim. (There isn't a record of many Muslim converts. Whether this means that more Christians became Jewish or that, for whatever reason, records of Muslim converts weren't made is not clear.) This Obadiah was made famous because of a letter Maimonides wrote to him. When rabbinic authorities answered letters about Jewish law, those answers were called *responsa* (singular, *responsum*). And Maimonides's letter to Obadiah the Proselyte is the most famous *responsum* of the medieval era. The legal matter is a complicated one. The question revolves around whether a convert can legitimately say such words as

"God of Our Fathers" in prayer when, of course, the convert's ancestors did not worship the God that Jewish ancestors worshipped. Maimonides, one of the most renowned and respected Jewish thinkers of all time, responded that converts could indeed utter the same words born Jews used and not change them in the least. Maimonides concluded that Abraham was the spiritual father of all converts. Maimonides directly stated that converts should not consider that their origins were inferior to that of born Jews, for all people ultimately were created by the one God.

It should be noted, however, that not all Jewish thinkers concluded that there was no difference at all between converts and born Jews. Yehuda Halevi, mentioned at the beginning of the book, respected converts but believed that there was a fundamental difference between someone born Jewish and someone who was not. He thought only Jews, because of some innate, inborn quality, could receive a revelation from God.

Many of these converts, perhaps fifteen thousand between 1000 and 1200, became Jewish and fled Christian Europe for Muslim areas.

In the twelfth century, Rabbenu Tam ruled that a local Jewish community should accept as a convert a man who had a romantic affair with a Jewish woman and wished to become Jewish so that he could marry the woman. Abraham ben Abraham was a former monk from Würzburg. He mistrusted the Bible translation he was given and decided that a true reading compelled him to become Jewish. In England, a Dominican friar named Robert of Reading supposedly converted because of his reading of Hebrew literature. He took the name Haggai and married a Jewish woman. Converts continued to be made in England until the expulsion of the Jews from that country in 1290. In fact, the expulsion order specifically mentioned that one of the reasons for the expulsion was that Jews were proselytizing.

For anyone who doubts Jewish conversionary zeal and what in our own era would be called chutzpah, should examine the life of Abraham Abulafia (1240–c. 1291). In the summer of 1280, Abulafia journeyed to Rome. His intention was to convert Pope Nicholas III to Judaism. Abulafia sought to see the pope on the eve of the Jewish New Year. The pope, however, was not in Rome; he was instead residing at his summer house. The pope had been informed of the conversionary plan before the journey and ordered Abulafia to be burned at the stake once he arrived in Rome. When Abulafia arrived at the outer gate of the pope's residence, he was not arrested, for during the night before, Nicholas had died of an apoplectic stroke. Abulafia was jailed for twenty-eight days and then released.

Besides a wide variety of individual converts, many of whom we most probably do not know because records were not kept, there were various group conversions. Without question, the most famous and the most intellectually consequential was the conversion of the Khazars.

The Khazars were a Turkic people. They lived in southern Russia between the Black and the Caspian Seas. As alluded to at the beginning of the book, the legend and Jewish writing has it that either in the eighth century (the date usually given is 740) or perhaps in the ninth century (the date here is given as 838), Bulan, the Khazar king, held a debate in which speakers for Judaism, Islam, and Christianity each presented their case for the king to accept the religion they represented. The legend that emerged was that Bulan was not satisfied with his ancestors' pagan religion. He had a dream in which great victories were promised if he would only embrace the one true religion. That is why he supposedly went in search of it and had the debate. On the basis of the arguments he heard, the legend continues, the king and his court chose Judaism. It is far more probable, however, that Jewish refugees, seeking escape from Byzantine persecution, moved to Kha-

zaria and intermarried. Or it was travelers, or traders, or a combi-
nation that introduced the Khazars to Judaism. Khazaria evidently
existed as a Jewish kingdom for perhaps 130 years. It is not clear,
and ultimately is the source of much confusion, exactly how many
people who lived in the kingdom converted. Did Bulan force
everyone to become Jewish? It seems more likely that Bulan and
the political elite adopted Judaism rather than the entire people.
Surely some people in the kingdom, seeing the religious behavior
of their leaders, wished to emulate it. But there is no evidence of
widespread forced conversion, and that seems like the sort of
political act that would have been recorded. There would likely,
for example, have been records of resistance to such an effort.
But since history is often written about the elite classes, it seems
more likely that only Bulan and perhaps a few of the leaders
became Jewish.

Why, then, did the legend persist among Jews that the entire
kingdom converted, or at least a large majority of the population?
To understand the answer to that question, it is necessary to com-
prehend the effect of the Khazars on medieval Jews. The Jews
were theologically desperate for an explanation of their condition.
They had lost their land and their Temple. They had seen two
religions arise and absorb converts they might have had. They
were landless and powerless, persecuted and forcibly converted.
Had God, they must have wondered, abandoned them? Was the
covenant over? It was the far future that became their explanation. One day God would redeem Jewish history. A Messiah
would come, and on that glorious day all the nations of the world
would, in the glare of divine truth, see the error of their ways and
embrace the Holy One, the God of Israel. In the meantime, to get
through the miserable years prior to the Messiah, the Jews
learned to judge themselves by their ability to observe religious
commandments and not by their success in the world.

The conversion of the Khazars was crucial to the shaping of this worldview because it served as an illustration to Jews of the genuine attractions of their religion and as a foretaste of what would one day come with the arrival of the Messiah. That is why, for example, Yehuda Halevi seized on the story of the Khazars when he wanted to offer an explanation of the condition of the Jews.

The Russians and the Byzantines attacked the Khazars, and their power declined. By the early eleventh century, the Russians dominated them.

It is the fate of the Khazars that has caused much confusion and much mischief in Jewish history. In the twentieth century, for example, there were about thirty thousand Mountain Jews who lived in Dagestan in the Russian Caucasus and in Azerbaijan who believed themselves to be directly descended from the Khazars.

But far more important is the startling thesis that the Khazars as a people converted to Judaism and that these people were the ancestors of Eastern Europe's Jews who did not, according to this theory, originate in the Land of Israel.

The standard historical theory is that Jews from Germany migrated eastward to Poland and Russia to form the basis of Eastern Europe's Jewish population. That standard view has been challenged on several grounds: that linguistically, Yiddish has Slavic origins, that demographically, the small number of Western Jews in medieval times could not account for the large number of Eastern European Jews, that Eastern European Jewish place names indicated a Khazarian origin, that genetic theory supports such a view, and so on.

The first reference to a supposed connection between the Khazars and Ashkenazic Jews was made by Rabbi Isaac Baer Levinsohn (1788–1860), but Abraham Eliyahu Harkavi's presentation of the idea in 1869 was much more widely read. The notion that Khazarian ancestors formed the majority of the Ashkenazic

Jewish population was developed by the French thinker Ernest Renan. Other writers followed suit, including, for example, H. G. Wells, who argued, in what would be the basis for later political dispute about the issue, that the Ashkenazi Jews did not originate in Judea. The Khazar-Ashkenazi Jewish connection became widely known in 1976 with the publication of *The Thirteenth Tribe* by Arthur Koestler. That book attracted wide attention because of Koestler's fame.

As mentioned earlier, the historian Shlomo Sand has made the idea current again in his book *The Invention of the Jewish People.* This book has the deliberate intention to undermine the Jewish claim to be descended from inhabitants of the Land of Israel and thus have the right to return there and re-form a Jewish nation.

Indeed, a wide variety of anti-Semites and anti-Zionists have seized upon the Khazar theory to undermine Jewish claims to Israel or their self-defined ancestry.

The principal scholarly conclusion, though, is that the story of the Khazars is in fact exaggerated, centered on the elite, and maybe even a created Jewish fable. As earlier noted, current DNA theory is generally assumed to be opposed to a Khazarian origin to Ashkenazi Jews and to support the notion that Ashkenazi Jews had Middle Eastern origins. There are historical documents that show Ashkenzi Jews in Germany in 321 CE, hundreds of years before the Khazar conversion.

The Khazars and other stories that went around the Jewish world affected Jewish thinkers. At least some Jewish thinkers in the medieval era continued to admire converts and see encouraging conversion as a Jewish mission, even as conversion was changing in Jewish life.

An important fourteenth-century Jewish philosopher named Hasdai Crescas could, for example, continue to claim that exile from the Promised Land still served a missionary purpose. Crescas wrote that God's name could be proclaimed in all the lands where the Jews lived, that the message of the prophets could be articulated by Jews in foreign lands. Crescas believed that as this religious truth of Judaism became known, all the nations of the world would embrace God.

The acceptance of converts can also be seen by the fact that prominent rabbis accepted those converts as rabbinic students. And some went even beyond that. Rabbi Shimon ben Zemach Duran of Rashbaz (1361–1444) believed that offering Judaism to Gentiles in order to encourage converts ought to be understood as one of the 613 biblical commandments. Indeed, the very fact that Jews continued to accept converts at a time when doing so endangered their personal and communal life is powerful evidence that some Jews at least considered the obligation to proselytize so great that physical danger could not be used as an excuse to halt such a godly enterprise.

Yet despite these remnants of support for assertive efforts to welcome converts, it should be noted that internally, Jewish behavior toward proselytizing was changing. Any interpretation of Jewish life must cohere with the reality Jews faced and the needs they had. And the reality was one of persecution and restrictions, of exile, of the triumph first of Christianity and then of Islam in attracting the very potential converts who might have become Jewish. The needs involved withdrawing from the world, preserving what still existed and could be preserved, and not provoking those with more power and an inclination to harm Jews who engaged in any provocations. The progression of the Middle Ages was matched by a progression in Jewish thought that for political and physical survival, segregation was the most beneficial approach to the Jewish condition.

Jews maintained religious authority within their own communities. They reinterpreted the notion of power to mean such religious authority. They had an important problem, though. If proselytizing continued to be seen as a religious obligation, then the delicate balance of their lives would be deeply disrupted. And so, over time, the Jewish attitude underwent a radical change because of external circumstances and community needs. The cognitive dissonance inherent in still believing in the required mission of proselytizing while needing to segregate was solved by redefining conversion as un-Jewish, as not required, as a Christian and Muslim activity, not a Jewish one.

It is this attitude, so at odds with authentic biblical, Greco-Roman, and crucial parts of Talmudic Judaism, that came to be defined as normal in Jewish life. Because the medieval era lasted for so long, this anticonversionary attitude came, falsely, to be understood as the genuinely Jewish attitude rather than one forced on the Jews.

The need for self-segregation, that is, had brought with it a justifying ideology that emphasized passivity, that focused exclusively on obeying ritual *mitzvot* (commandments), that waited anxiously for the coming arrival of the Messiah, who would usher in a great era in Jewish life. This was a difficult way in which to live and in part explains why Jews were so eager to welcome so many of the false messiahs who litter Jewish history. The future life they envisioned was much more satisfying than the real life they endured.

It should also be added that Jews saw potential converts in a new way. As Christian hostility toward and persecution of Jews continued and then intensified, Jews understandably became suspicious of all Christians. It became psychologically ever more difficult for Jews to offer conversion to the very people who were persecuting them, mocking them, forcibly converting them, injuring them, and even killing them. The very idea of a mission to the Gentiles understandably became more and more emotionally repugnant.

The spiraling decline of conversion to Judaism had other reasons as well. Most religious Christians of the era believed the

Jews guilty of deicide and disavowed by God. They were hardly a people to join. Their religion, it was thought, had been superseded, and they had been tossed into the dustbin of religious history. For their part, as Jews engaged in ever-increasing self-restrictive behavior, they made religious rules more rigid. They became less willing to adjust their requirements and rituals to allow additional conversions to Judaism. The Jewish people had by tradition been divided, with lots of groups having a variety of approaches. In the Middle Ages, there became one Judaism, not many. Ironically, this Judaism became identified as the genuine, the solely acceptable Judaism until the rise of modern times and the emergence of the more common Jewish historical experience of a variety of approaches to Judaism. Additionally, Jews simply didn't believe that Gentiles would join a persecuted people, and purity of motive was a requirement for conversion.

Despite the one Judaism in Jewish ritual practice, there did continue to linger some disputes about the nature of conversion. There were two kinds of teachers of the Halakhah in the second half of the thirteenth century. One school wished to explain the Talmud and other classic texts the rabbis had written. These teachers were termed *mefareshim*, or commentators, and their job was to establish the laws that could be used in everyday life. The principal commentators were centered in areas under Christian rule, such as France and Germany. The great scholar Rashi (1040–1105) was one of these. Rashi's two sons-in-law began the school of the Tosafists, about three hundred scholars who lived between the twelfth and the fourteenth centuries. They wrote *tosafot*, or additions, to thirty of the Talmud's tractates. They created questions, rulings, interpretations, notes, and other additions to Rashi's running commentary on the Talmud.

The Tosafists were profoundly in favor of proselytes. Rashi, for example, in his comments on Deuteronomy 33:19 and Isaiah 44:4–5, observed that redemption for the Jews would be preceded by converts joining the Jewish people. The Tosafists were the first to say directly that Jewish law required that converts be accepted. In a way, the commandment to proselytize was the basis of the Tosafist interpretations of the Talmud.

The other group of teachers were known as *posekim*, or the decision makers. They were primarily located in Spain, North Africa, and other areas that were under Muslim control. Their religious focus was on writing legal codes and response. Maimonides was the most famous of the *posekim*; he compiled the classic Jewish code the Mishneh Torah. In general, the *posekim* was not as open to converts or proselytization as the Tosafists, although, as has been noted, Maimonides was generous to converts themselves if not to the Jewish community actively proselytizing.

Because both schools existed with conflicting views about conversion, it is no surprise that there was considerable communal confusion.

A man named Asher ben Jehiel tried to produce a legal code that would balance the views of the two conflicting schools. There were various other attempts to blend these two very different systems of the law.

In a way, unsurprisingly, because the law followed the Jewish condition of the time so closely, the evolving law made proselytizing more and more restricting. Especially in the era after the Fourth Lateran Council of 1215, when there was an active and quite vicious campaign against Jewish efforts to win converts, the codifiers felt a vital need to protect the community, to focus on survival and maintenance, not growth and mission, and to sacrifice Jewish universalism in favor of a prudential particularism.

It was in this environment that the most famous code was produced. Joseph Caro existed when there were many conflicting views about Jewish law. He sought to unify these views and wrote the Shulhan Arukh (1564–1565), which sought to use the opinion of the majority but favored the *posekim* with their restrictive conversionary views. It was when Moses Isserles added notes to Caro in 1569–1571 that the Shulhan Arukh became the Jewish community's authoritative code, perhaps at least in part because it was the first Jewish legal code that was produced after the invention of the printing press and so was more widely available and capable of being distributed quickly.

The Shulhan Arukh became, in effect, the official code, the defining legal document of Jewish life. Its historical effect, then, is impossible to overstate. For centuries, Jewish legal authorities and Jewish communities identified Judaism with the rules as expounded in the Shulhan Arukh.

It is crucial, then, to examine what the Shulhan Arukh said about converts. The subject is covered in the section Yoreh De'ah, chapters 268–69. That is, there is only a relatively brief discussion of the subject. It had evidently become much less important in the Jewish life of the day. Caro quotes Maimonides and seems to be opposed to any active efforts to welcome converts. But the subject is complicated. The very fact that Caro presents laws for proselytes and does so in a way more favorable than Maimonides, indicates that however difficult it was for Jews to accept converts, they continued to find a legal way to do so. Given the times, that is, the Shulhan Arukh is pro-conversionary. Caro did not quote the Talmudic statement that converts are like sores and did include some Tosafist opinion. Indeed, in Yoreh De'ah chapter 268, Caro writes that those who wish to convert should be told at some length that the idolatrous nations of the world will perish but that the people Israel will surely survive and that one day Judaism will become the sole religion of the world. (Caro uses Yevamot 47a from the Talmud as the source for this opinion.) In some ways, Caro is preserving the possibility for proselytizing once the situation of the Jews improves, once the legislation forbidding conversion no longer exists. Caro might have simply forbidden all conversions. But he still saw converts as acceptable in principle.

However generously Caro is read, however, it is clear that the Tosafist interpretation of proselytizing as a religious commandment has disappeared from Jewish religious life. This was compounded by some in the community using a very narrow interpretation of Caro to be wary of converts or to forbid receiving them.

The irony was overwhelming. Encouraging converts, which once was central to the Jewish mission in history, once widely practiced, became identified as un-Jewish, as antithetical to the idea of Judaism as being essentially about obeying Jewish ritual commandments such as keeping the Sabbath or keeping kosher.

Once seeking converts was no longer seen as a religious obligation, its demise was inevitable. For Jews might feel obligated to seek converts even when doing so endangered them and their community if such as effort was seen as divinely obligatory. But if seeking converts was not a commandment, and if it was dangerous, and for all the other reasons mentioned, the Jewish view toward converts had turned 180 degrees to one of negative reaction.

Any changes would have to occur in a new historical era.

5

LEAVING THE GHETTO

Converts from the Jewish Englightenment
to the Present

The Middle Ages ended in Western Europe with the arrival of the Renaissance, the cultural rebirth that began in Italy in the late fourteenth century and eventually spread elsewhere. For the Jewish people, however, their entry into modernity was delayed because they mostly resided in Eastern Europe in what is now Poland and the countries of the former Soviet Union.

The Jewish emergence into an enlightened era had to wait until the aftermath of the French Revolution, which began in 1789. Before then, however, Eastern Europe was the scene of a Catholic backlash against the emergence of Protestant power in the West. This is best illustrated by the case of Catherine Zaleshovska in 1539. Catherine, age eighty, was the wife of an alderman in Cracow. She was accused of following the Jewish religion secretly. Peter Gamrat, the bishop of Cracow, headed the court that tried her. When the court asked her whether she believed in God's son, Jesus Christ, she responded that God did not have either a wife or son. The court found her guilty of blasphemy. She was sent to the city jail, and she was burned several days later in Cracow's marketplace.

Wild rumors spread throughout Poland based on this case. It was said that Cracow's Christians especially were converting to Judaism and then being taken to Lithuania, where the Jews there hid them. When this rumor proved immune to factual inquiry, another rumor began. In this one, many Lithuanian Jews were going to emigrate to Turkey, taking the Christian converts with them. The sultan in Turkey, the rumor continued, was aiding in this effort. This rumor, too, proved false, but it illustrates the tensions between Jews and Christians lingering at the dawn of the modern era.

In Hungary, the opposite of what had occurred in Poland took place. Suleiman the Magnificent, the sultan of Turkey, conquered much of the world around Hungary in 1541, except Transylvania. The sultan treated Hungary's Jews very well, but he persecuted Hungary's Christians mercilessly. In reaction, many Hungarian Christians embraced Judaism in order to attain the relatively better status that Jews enjoyed.

In Transylvania, still free, the religious situation evolved into one of great tolerance. Following the normal historical pattern of encouraging converts when they were free to do so, the Jews of Transylvania began a successful campaign to win new adherents. There were also many people there who admired Judaism but did not wish to be identified with such persecuted people as Jews. Many of these people became Unitarians. It was one of these Unitarians, named Andreas Eossi, who was chancellor of Transylvaia from 1588 to 1623 and who started a new religious sect. Its followers, like their Russian counterparts, were known as Sabbatarians. They kept the Jewish dietary laws. They observed the Sabbath on Saturdays. They observed many Jewish holy days. Eossi's adopted son, Simon Pechi, succeeded his father and decided to become fully Jewish. Pechi reportedly won twenty thousand converts, although that most likely is a highly exaggerated number, but it indicates that more than a few people did become Jewish.

However, when Prince George II Rákóczi ascended to head the kingdom, the rights that Jews had enjoyed were revoked. Again following what began to look like a historical law, in dangerous times of persecution the Jews withdrew from active proselytizing efforts. Pechi was removed from his office and tossed into prison. He escaped and went to Constantinople, where he translated religious works from Hebrew into Hungarian.

There is another important group of Jews, some of whom engaged in efforts to encourage converts. These were the *anusim* ("forced" in Hebrew), more commonly known as Marranos or Conversos (the converted). The *anusim* lived in Spain and Portugal and, if they did not go involuntarily into exile, were forced to become Christians in Spain in 1492 and in Portugal in 1497. Some of these *anusim* continued to observe Jewish ritual laws in secret.

That led in some cases to a sad consequence. Diogo da Assumpção, for example, was born in Viana, Portugal, in 1579. He became a monk and took a special interest in the Hebrew Bible because of a family story that several generations earlier a converted Jew had entered into marriage with a member of the family. After much study, he concluded that Judaism was the true religion. He planned to flee Portugal, but he was betrayed, arrested, and imprisoned. He was brought before the Inquisition but refused to recant his beliefs. Instead he spent time in prison as one of the *anusim*, fasting on Fridays, as was their custom. It was on August 3, 1603, that Diogo, age twenty-four, was burned alive in Lisbon. Portuguese *anusim* formed a group in his honor named "The Brotherhood of Saint Diogo."

Francisco Maldonado da Silva lived in Peru. The surgeon was a descendant of *anusim*. Ironically, he became particularly interested in Judaism after reading a book meant to illustrate the falsity of Judaism. He became Jewish and tried to convert his sisters. One of them denounced him to the Inquisition, and he was arrested in 1627. Sent to Lima for a trial, he became subject to theologians trying to convince him of the error of his ways. One day, he crept through the window of his cell. But da Silva did not attempt to escape. Instead, he went to the Christian prisoners in adjoining cells and tried to get them to convert to Judaism.

Recaptured, he took to writing. He made his ink from charcoal, his pen a chicken bone cut with a knife made from a nail. He found scraps of paper where he could and wrote more than two hundred pages outlining his religious beliefs. Together with six other *anusim* who refused to denounce Judaism, he was burned alive on January 23, 1639.

Beyond the return to Judaism in Europe, there were also stories of people without Jewish ancestry or family connection becoming Jewish. Consider the case of Conrad Victor. He was a professor at the University of Marburg, where he taught classical languages. In 1607, determined to become Jewish, Victor immigrated to Salonica in Greece. There he joined the Jewish people, taking the name Moses Prado. Nicholas Antoine was born in 1602 in Briey in France. He decided to leave Catholicism and become a Protestant minister. It was only after he entered the ministry that he found Judaism to be enormously attractive. Antoine approached the rabbis in Metz seeking to convert, but they refused to convert him. Undeterred, he traveled to Venice, but the rabbis there also refused him, scared evidently of the possible repercussions to the Jewish community because Esther, a woman who had converted, had recently been burned at the stake in Venice. The rabbis told Antoine to go to Padua. The rabbis there advised him to remain a Christian, and he returned to Switzerland. There, he was publicly a minister, but he privately practiced Judaism. His interpretations of biblical texts and religious behavior eventually aroused suspicion, and he was arrested for heresy. When he finally openly announced that he had become Jewish, the charge against him was changed from heresy—to lunacy. When he refused to give up Judaism, the heresy charge was reinstated. His trial began on April 11, 1632. On April 20, he was sentenced to be strangled and have his body burned at the stake. The sentence was carried out that same day.

The Jewish scholars and leaders, when they learned of such stories, which did not always occur, had various reactions to conversion in this era. Rabbi Samuel Eliezer Edels, for example, kept a quotation from the biblical book of Job over the entrance to his house. The quotation (Job 31:32) stated that the stranger (the word *ger* in Hebrew, which was later understood to mean "convert") did not stay in the street, but rather the speaker kept the door open for the stranger. Leo da Modena, who lived in Venice, took note of Rabbi Helbo's statement in the Talmud about converts being as difficult as a sore. Da Modena said the words Helbo spoke were made at a time when the Jewish people wished to remain apart from others, but that time had passed and converts were to be more welcome.

One historically interesting case of how conversion affected the policies of nations toward the Jews can be seen in the case of Rabbi Manasseh ben Israel (1604–1657), a descendant of the *anusim*. Manasseh was a mystic, believing that the long-awaited still-tarrying Messiah would not arrive until the Jews were scattered to every corner of the earth. Using his own calculations, he concluded that they had reached everywhere except England, a country from which the Jews had been expelled in 1290. Deciding that it was his task to hasten the arrival of the Messiah, Manasseh decided to persuade Lord Protector Oliver Cromwell and the British parliament to allow the Jews to return. Cromwell listened to the request but then told Manasseh that there were objections to the Jews; namely, the charges that they used the blood of

Christian children to make matzoh at Passover, that they charged excessive interest for loans and through this usury bankrupted countries where they lived, and that they constantly attempted to convert Christians to Judaism. The last complaint was an especially sore one for Cromwell since some fellow Puritans had gone to Holland and converted to Judaism. Manasseh stated the first charge was completely ridiculous, that Jews wouldn't have to be moneylenders if they were allowed to participate in all trades, and that seeking converts was antithetical to Judaism. Since Manasseh knew the last point was false, the only logical explanation is that he assumed making such a statement would allow the Jews back in England and usher in the Messiah's return, and with that return, all Gentiles would follow the faith of the one true God. Manasseh promised that if the Jews were allowed back to England they would not try to convince anyone to convert to Judaism. This promise had repercussions. British Jews throughout the empire made conversion very difficult.

In 1751, for example, some Norwegian Christians arrived in London seeking to become Jewish. The leaders at the Spanish and Portuguese synagogue turned them down and sent letters to other synagogues asking that they also refuse any conversionary request. This led to a proclamation read in all of London's synagogues promising expulsion and the refusal of any religious requests to any congregant who sought to entice a Christian to become Jewish.

It is in this context that the case of Lord George Gordon is particularly interesting. Gordon was born in London on December 26, 1751. King George II was his godfather. Gordon served in the navy, and then he returned to Scotland, where he had been brought up. He was elected to the British House of Commons in 1774. Among his political views, Gordon was an ardent champion of the American Revolution. Throughout his life, Gordon was also ardent about another, more religious position: he was virulently anti-Catholic, so much so that he organized and became president of the United Protestant League, a society with the specific purpose of preventing Catholics from keeping the political rights they had gained in the Catholic Relief Act of 1778. Gordon worked to have the act repealed.

There was a huge anti-Catholic rally in London on June 2, 1780. Gordon led the sixty thousand people in attendance. The crowd began to march from St. George's Fields to the Houses of Parliament in order to present their petition. They reached Westminster. What was later called the "Gordon Riots" commenced. The mob first threatened to push their way into the House of Commons. Then, over the next several days, they took to destroying Roman Catholic chapels, attacked Catholics in their homes, broke open various prisons and set fire to Newgate Prison, and attacked various public buildings, including the Bank of England. Before the army could end the riots, an estimated 450 people were killed or wounded.

Gordon was arrested on June 9 and charged with inciting a riot and high treason. He was put in the Tower of London. The Reverend John Wesley, leader of the Methodists, was among Gordon's visitors. Gordon was acquitted of both charges at his trial on the basis that he had not intended to commit treason. Several prominent people, including the author Samuel Johnson, applauded the acquittal. Charles Dickens wrote about the riots in his novel *Barnaby Rudge*. Dickens seems to imply that Gordon had an early interest in Judaism.

Gordon's legal troubles, though, were not yet over. In June 1787, he was tried and convicted of libel. After the conviction, he approached Rabbi David Tevele Schiff, asking to be converted to Judaism. His motives are not entirely clear. Perhaps he simply found the Jewish faith more appealing than his own. But the British custom prevailed, and Rabbi Schiff turned him down. Gordon then went to Amsterdam, but the British asked for his return since he was simply free on bail. He went back to Birmingham, where a Rabbi Jacob completed the conversion.

On December 7, 1787, he was ordered to begin his sentence in Newgate Prison. He continued to lead the life of a religious Jew in prison. He organized a prayer group on the Sabbath from among the various Polish Jewish prisoners.

Many prominent Jews, shocked at some of his views and behavior, tried to disavow Gordon. Rumors were spread that he was insane. Poorer Jews continued to find him a fascinating figure, this once powerful man who had abandoned Protestantism and lived a strictly Jewish life. In *Barnaby Rudge*, Dickens describes this period in prison in sympathetic language: "The prisoners bemoaned his loss, and missed him, for though his means were not large his charity was great, and in bestowing alms among them he considered the necessities of all alike, and knew no distinction of sect or creed."

Gordon was set to be released on June 29, 1793, but the release was conditioned on a person with means guaranteeing appropriate future behavior. There was no such person. Rich Jews disdained him. The court did not accept the poor Jews who appeared with him because they had no money.

He was therefore forced to go back to prison, although at some level it seems he wished to return there because he turned down the help of his brothers and sisters. In October 1793 he caught typhoid fever, and he died on November 1. He was forty-one.

As in the case of the Puritans Oliver Cromwell disliked, and as George Gordon tried to do, many people came to Amsterdam to convert. Moses ben Abraham Avinu Haas, for example, converted in 1686 or 1687, married the daughter of a rabbi, and was a publisher of many Hebrew and Yiddish books.

Johann Peter Spaeth was a Catholic, turned Lutheran, turned Catholic again. His embrace of Judaism came about because of an accident. A crucifix once fell out of his pocket. A Jewish man picked up the cross and saw in it the face of the Jewish peoples' sorrows. Spaeth wrote that the Jew's words brought about a sudden new grasp of the fifty-third chapter of the book of Isaiah. Spaeth claims the incident made him believe that it was the Jews who bore the sins for the Gentiles who persecuted them on a daily basis. Spaeth realized how badly Christians had treated Jews, and it was out of that realization that he determined Christianity was fraudulent and he had to leave it. Spaeth converted and took the name Moses Germanus, Moses the German.

Israel ben Abraham Avinu, or alternately Israel Ger or Israel the Convert, had been a monk. He wrote attacks on his former religion. He established publishing businesses.

The story of Russia's Jews during this era is a strange one and does involve conversion. During the rule of Peter the Great (1682–1725), there were almost no Jews living in the Russian Empire. Only in Smolensk, near the border with Poland, was there a small Jewish community. The Jews there were tax and customs collectors for various nobles. Baruch Leibov was one of these collectors. Leibov used some of his earnings to build a synagogue, an undertaking that infuriated a local Greek Orthodox priest, who claimed the synagogue was the first step in a Jewish plot to convert the whole community to Judaism. Empress Catherine, who succeeded Peter, issued a rule in March 1727 that Jews were to be deported. But Leibov was undeterred. The expulsion had allowed Jews to visit Russia for business reasons, and Leibov was one of those who returned. It was during one of his business trips that Leibov met Alexander Voznitzin, who had once served as a captain in the Russian navy. Voznitzin was a dedicated student of the Bible and wished to study the Hebrew language. He asked Leibov to teach the language and the basics of Judaism to him. In 1738, Voznitzin's wife denounced her husband as being a convert. She particularly mentioned Leibov as the man who had tricked her husband. Both men were arrested. Their trial began on March 22, 1738. The two men were tortured and "confessed" that Voznitzin had indeed become Jewish. At eight o'clock in the morning on Saturday (the Jewish Sabbath), July 15, 1738, in St. Petersburg's public square, the two men were tied to a stake and killed.

Nahida Ruth Remy Lazarus, who had been born Nahida Strumhoefel in 1849 in Berlin, was originally Protestant. She was an early proponent of feminism, and in her book *Ich Suchte Sich* (*My Search*), she recalls that at age ten she read both biblical testaments and recoiled especially at Paul's attitude toward women. She refused to be confirmed as a Lutheran. Left a widow, she consulted a famous Berlin psychologist named Moritz Lazarus. Under his tutelage, she studied some of the most prominent Jewish thinkers of the generation. It was after she read Moses Mendelssohn's book *Jerusalem* that she decided to become Jewish. She intended to travel to Geneva to complete her formal conversion there and decided to stop at Freiburg on her journey to see Lazarus, who had become sick while on vacation. Lazarus got better, helped Nahida in her conversion, and then married her. Nahida Lazarus wrote a book about prayers and another book titled *Das Juedische Weib* (*The Jewish Woman*), which argued that Jewish attitudes toward women had always been favorable. She went on to write many more novels, essays, and stories as well as editing and publishing Lazarus's memoirs after his death.

As is currently the case, more women than men converted to Judaism. Yelizaveta Ivanovna Zhirkova (1889–1949), known as Elisheva in the canon of Hebrew literature, was a great writer. Her mother was English, her father a Greek Orthodox living in Russia. She spent her youth in Moscow and felt close to a religious Jewish family she knew and the Zionist passions of students she studied with. She was drawn to Jewish languages and studied both Hebrew and Yiddish. Eventually she began translating works in these Jewish languages into Russian. It was when she married Simon

Bychowsky, a Hebrew writer, that she began using the name Elisheva as her pen name. She formally converted to Judaism and found herself drawn more and more toward the magnetic attractions of the Zionist movement. She moved to Israel, where she lived until a year after the establishment of the nation.

Besides formal conversions to Judaism, there were interesting cases of people who didn't formally convert but who nevertheless became inordinately close to the Jewish people. Aimé Pallière (1873–1949), from France, is one of those people. For a while his attachment to Judaism was so close that he served as an assistant rabbi at a synagogue in Paris. He grew up in Lyon. His interest in Judaism began one evening when he was with a friend and they heard an alluring chant coming from a synagogue. Reared as a devout Catholic, he knew he wasn't supposed to participate in the services of another faith, but he could not resist. It was nearing the end of Yom Kippur, and the congregation was praying the closing service. Pallière was overwhelmed by the vitality of the praying, by what he thought of as the ancient genius of the Jewish people. He began studying Hebrew, and eventually went through a profound religious search. His mother's objections made him destroy the phylacteries he had made with his own hands. (These are tefillin, a leather box that Jews wear at morning prayer.) But Pallière continued to study Hebrew and Jewish history. He particularly became deeply disturbed by what he read of the Inquisition. Despite his dissatisfaction with Christianity, what he heard from rabbis did not please him either. At least that was so until he came in contact with Rabbi Elijah Benamozegh, the chief rabbi in Leghorn, Italy. The two began to correspond. Pallière wanted to be accepted as a Jew, but Rabbi Benamozegh discouraged him, saying that for what he wanted there was no need to have to adhere to all of Judaism's laws. Pallière, the rabbi suggested, could lead a noble life without a formal conversion, without having to obey each and every law as the Jews were required to do, according to strictly traditional views.

Pallière became, at least informally, a Noahide, a righteous Gentile who followed the seven laws of Noah, the moral rules the Talmud says are binding for all humanity. Six of these seven laws are that idolatry, murder, theft, sexual immorality, blasphemy, and eating any flesh of a living animal are prohibited. The seventh law is that courts have to be established to maintain law. Pallière was arrested and imprisoned by the Nazis when they occupied Paris. His story is told in his magnificent book *The Unknown Sanctuary: A Pilgrimage from Rome to Israel.*

All these conversions took place in a certain Jewish religious context. For Jews, the transformation from living in the Middle Ages to living in a modern age was marked by two principal effects: secularization and legal emancipation. The Jewish Enlightenment, known as Haskalah, took place in the eighteenth and nineteenth centuries among Europe's Jews. The Maskilim, leaders of this Jewish Enlightenment, wanted Jews to adopt the lessons from the wider European Enlightenment, especially grounding ideas in reason and promoting freedom of thought. This, of course, was a direct challenge to the rabbinic tradition that had guided Jewish life for so many centuries. The Jewish Enlightenment also focused on moving Jews out of the ghetto and making them participants in the wider societies around them. Advocates wanted to get away from a strictly Talmudic education and include a variety of secular studies and use of secular languages. Hebrew was emphasized, as was Jewish history. Jews reacted very differently to the Haskalah, with the end result being the division of Jews into different groups, one of which became known as the Orthodox, those who wished to retain the Jewish traditions that some modernist Jews wished to reject. Reform Judaism evolved from those Jews who wished to embrace modernity. Conservative

Judaism later came about because of what was viewed as Reform's excessive shedding of Jewish traditions.

Legal emancipation meant that the Jews of Western Europe (and America) were granted the civil rights accorded other citizens. In a way, the Haskalah was an internal emancipation, freeing the Jewish mind to choose to abandon the bonds of tradition. Legal emancipation was the external version of that freedom. From the late eighteenth century up to the early twentieth century, Jews in Europe began to be recognized as citizens with equality to other citizens. The long legacy of laws of discrimination were repealed or replaced. In practice, the legal rights accorded the Jews meant they could more fully participate in the social, commercial, and political lives of their society. They could physically move from restricted locations to integrate with their fellow citizens. They could move to countries, especially Great Britain and the countries in the Americas, where they were afforded even greater opportunities.

These modernist revolutions had a profound effect on Jews and conversion, or at least on some Jews.

The very notion of "Orthodox" Jews was born in the aftermath of the Haskalah and the emergence of those who broke away from tradition. Because the Orthodox were those Jews who wished to maintain the rabbinic traditions precisely as they had been followed, the Orthodox psychological strategy was to pretend that the religious changes going on all around them were not, in fact, occurring. Their only concern was maintaining what they knew, and the outside world's wild currents were only to be kept away by that fence around the Torah suggested in the Talmud. Of course, the Orthodox were intelligent and grasped the roller coaster of political activities. These, though, were in a sense gratefully accepted because the emancipation the changes brought relieved suffering. But the Orthodox still felt they were in exile from the Holy Land and therefore still eagerly awaited the arrival of the Messiah to bring them back. In that sense, their real emancipation had not come about at all. And so they carried on their religious tasks as before.

Those Jews who wished religious reform to mirror the political and intellectual upheavals going on around them—those, that is, who formed what became Reform Judaism—had a very different reaction than did the Orthodox. For them the very idea of exile disappeared. Unsurprisingly, then, one of the identifying marks of the original Reformers was that they excised from their prayer-books all mention of a Messiah coming to bring all the Jews back to the Promised Land. The Reform Jews concluded from their surroundings that they were German—the place Reform Judaism began—and not going to an ancient homeland. This insight, however, had its own implications. Before Haskalah, the Jews had a passive political goal—pray and wait. For the Reformers, that goal was so longer tenable. They were robbed, almost without noticing, of a political identity along with a traditional religious identity, which they did recognize, and they were eager to structure a new religious self.

The Reform Jews saw themselves and their condition in a new way. They were not awaiting a return but belonged where they were because they were part of a universal religious group. That group had to have a religious purpose, one that the centuries of exile had prepared them to undertake. It should be noted, as has been mentioned, that universality can be derived from Talmudic texts, that serving God can be derived from Isaiah's notion of the Jews as "suffering servants." Therefore, Reformers didn't see themselves as in any way leaving Judaism, only as interpreting its teachings in a new way, one more coherent with their actual situation.

Reform developed the idea of a mission, a sense of having a universalist message of a moral God that it could bring to the world. The Reformers asserted that Judaism would be more attractive if its religious adherents accepted universally recognized moral values and presented itself to the world in a way that would be more familiar than the traditional Jewish ways, which frequently seemed strange to outsiders. The Reformers wanted Gentiles to feel more comfortable with the outer face of Judaism in order to embrace its inner moral core. The particularist elements of Judaism were deemphasized. The rules of keeping kosher were a major source of separation between Jews and Gentiles, and so the Reformers eventually abandoned those rules. The Reformers cut their side curls, learned the secular language, and declared Jewish law no longer binding. Certain universal moral teachings embodied by the prophets were proclaimed as the very heart and soul of Judaism.

Reformers made two miscalculations. First, they promulgated a liberal universalism instead of a specifically Jewish universalism, one more grounded in Jewish roots, more politically sophisticated about the elements necessary for the mission's success. They might, at that historic juncture, still have maintained attachment to Jewish law but reinterpreted it, embraced Jewish nationalism, and maintained the particularist ceremonies.

Their second mistake came in their understanding of mission and the methods by which it should be undertaken. In a way, the Reform movement secularized the idea of Messiah that they rejected. In rejecting chosenness, the Reformers found a replacement in the idea that every people had its own unique mission and that the Jewish mission was to advance the social condition of humanity by making all people adhere to the prophetic ideals of Judaism. By eliminating Judaism's otherness in terms of dress, ritual, and belief, the Reformers were convinced that they had formed a religion that not only could better humanity but could be embraced by all humanity. Their intellectual error was that they weren't really bringing Gentiles to Judaism but to an already identified and accepted moral system stipulated as Judaism. Liberal Gentiles already friendly to Judaism—that is, the perfect candidates for conversion—already accepted these moral principles and already were willing to fight for the same sort of social betterment the Reformers wanted. These Gentiles, therefore, understandably saw no need to call themselves Jewish. Ironically, had they been offered some of the particulars the Reformers rejected, these Gentiles might have been more willing to change.

Even with these intellectual mistakes, the Reformers were still doomed to fail in making Judaism universal. For their "mission" turned out to be passive. They waited for the Gentiles to come to them. There were no missionaries, just beliefs in the rightness of their cause. The Gentiles did not arrive.

But these Reformers had made a major contribution. They reintroduced the dormant idea of mission back into Jewish life after centuries of that idea being missing. Without these early Reformers, such an idea would not have returned.

To put it mildly, these Reform movement ideas were not met with universal acceptance. The traditionalists saw the Reformers thinning Judaism, making it into a set of theological assertions, most of which were already accepted by the Gentile world and others that Gentiles would not, in the traditionalists' view, take seriously. The Reformers, that is, were charged with offering an inauthentic Judaism to a Gentile audience that wouldn't even want that. Worse, the traditionalists claimed, was that the Reformers were offering a way station on the journey to full assimilation, pretending to offer a truly Jewish view that was not. It was inevitable, the Orthodox claimed, that those who started on this journey to assimilation would complete it. And it seemed especially paradoxical to the Orthodox that such a dilution of Judaism was accompanied by a mission to offer that diluted view to the world.

These were powerful charges, but they weren't entirely fair. After all, the Reformers played a crucial role in Jewish history.

The Enlightenment accompanied by emancipation in theory and in practice made full assimilation a highly attractive possibility for the Jews who had been trapped in ghettos, deprived of economic and educational opportunities and cut off from the wider societies around them. Assimilation was a glittering prize, and many Jews reached for it.

It was the Reformers that kept many Jews from assimilating by offering them a chance to stay Jewish but have a genuine taste of modernity. There were, after all, no more communal capabilities to stop any Jew from leaving the community. On the contrary, there were powerful forces luring Jews away from their Judaism. A Christian identity gave them passage everywhere. Such an identity provided vocational opportunities in places where employers remained anti-Jewish. It gave them romantic opportunities and political ones. As the born-Jewish but converted poet Heinrich Heine exemplified and put it, becoming Christian offered a ticket to all of Europe's culture.

In brief, the Reformers were very clever in seeing the need for some way to keep these Jews Jewish. All the Jews had to do, the Reformers concluded, was to have Jewish beliefs. Their mission idea was legitimate and sincere.

The Orthodox also missed an important element. The connection made by the Reformers between theology and mission had been part of traditional Judaism as well. Traditional Judaism had a vision of the end times, the arrival of the Messiah, the return to the Land of Israel, a time of peace when all the peoples of the world would come under the wings of the divine. The problem for the Orthodox was that such a moment was in the future. They therefore needed a plan to survive as Jews until the Messiah arrived. That plan was a form of mission. All religious thinking, that is, requires the concept of mission. The Reformers had simply adapted it as they had so much else for the modern age. They had excluded the idea of a Messiah and had reinterpreted all of the Jewish past as an offering of a universal mission.

The Reformers were misled by history. They were convinced that the world would come to Judaism because they saw before their eyes an incredible amount of social progress. Democratic institutions arose where they hadn't before. The idea of equality took root. There were movements for social improvement. Later, in the last quarter of the nineteenth century and the first decade of the twentieth, there was an immense number of inventions. Just in those few years, for example, consider what was invented: the phonograph, the electric light, the telegraph, motion pictures, the automobile, the airplane, and the all-electric television tube were just some of the inventions. Is it any wonder that prior to the First World War people could believe in the inevitable progress of humanity?

The Reformers in performing their mission made enormous changes in Jewish rituals. Circumcisions were dispensed with as a requirement for male converts. It was enough for converts to make a statement affirming their belief in God, in the brotherhood of humanity (the language of the day was still sexist), and in the Jewish mission. The Reformers in various places eliminated holidays, reduced the amount of Hebrew in the service as being unattractive to Gentiles, and eliminated the need to wear a *kippah*, a head covering. The idea of keeping kosher was eliminated.

Ironically, despite all these changes designed to make Judaism more comprehensible and attractive to Gentiles, the idea of mission failed. The conversions that did occur did not take place because Gentiles became attracted to Jewish theological propositions but because Gentiles became attracted to Jewish romantic partners. Marriage, not belief systems, created conversions.

Why did the mission idea end up having so little impact? As mentioned, the Reform movement did little to create institutional structures through which to undertake the mission. Reformers talked about it. They wrote about it. They preached about it. But they rarely found a way to put it into practice. Part of this was the very theology the Reform movement accepted. They were religiously tolerant. They never thought and certainly never claimed that Judaism was the only way to reach heaven. Becoming Jewish was not a requirement for salvation. The Reformers had a deep intellectual desire for a mission, but they lacked the fervor, the fire in every vein, that comes with a certainty of religious belief matched by a felt need to save others. Judaism simply didn't have such a view, and so its adherents never felt the missionary fervor that, for example, Christians and Muslims of the day constantly experienced. The Reformers, ironically, did exactly what the Orthodox did. They didn't reach out to their neighbors to effect a conversion. They served as passive moral models who hoped their example would serve as an inspiration to the Gentiles around them.

The Reformers, in diluting Judaism so far, did in fact the opposite of what they intended. They made it difficult, for example, to explain how they differed from the Unitarians beyond history. They walked their own followers up to the doorstep of assimilation. In time, the Reform movement, like every successful movement, would engage in a series of self-correcting moves, but at the beginning their mission idea didn't work, except in the one crucial way of reintroducing the idea of encouraging converts to Judaism, an idea by then distant and foreign to the Jewish mind.

There remained an additional problem as well. The early Reform movement concluded that the Jews were no longer a nation. Reformers did not yearn, in theory, for a return to their ancient homeland. Their lands of residence were the New Jerusalem. This might have cohered with the Talmudic observation of Diaspora life as an impetus to seek converts. But the Reform movement was stuck with another problem. It couldn't make Judaism exactly parallel to Christianity, even with changing the rituals and even with giving up the idea of returning to some national state. Judaism was not simply a group of beliefs. Jews were a people. If a person became a Christian, the person accepted a closed set of theological propositions and joined a religious movement. There could be no parallel because of the complexity of conversion to Judaism. It didn't just involve the embrace of a religion or way of life. It involved joining a new people.

Jewish tradition has always suggested it is possible to do that, not just to switch beliefs and practices but also to become part of the Jewish people. That is because the notion of "people" was separate from the idea of either nation or genetic inheritance. And that is because conceiving of Judaism as a "religion" misses a key component of its meaning.

It is in the post-Jewish Enlightenment period when Orthodoxy defined itself, when Reform and Conservative Judaism came to be, that Judaism through its own effort to become accepted as part of Christian Europe, to define itself as a "religion" therefore confused efforts to clarify conversion.

Into this heady mix of freedom, the swirling nationalisms of Europe, the increasing secularism of the world, and the rise of science came the emergence of racism and with it the partial transformation of hatred of the Jews from a purely religious hatred to include a "racial" hatred, a view that supplemented the traditional religious hatred.

Alongside all this, the Jews were intermingling with Gentiles, meeting them for the first time or at least genuinely talking to them as political equals for the first time. This emancipation of the Jews led to an unexpected phenomenon: Jews and Gentiles fell in love and intermarried. Those relationships became a major focus in the later history of the Jewish people.

The rates of interfaith marriages between European Jews and Christians accelerated during the nineteenth century and particularly in the early twentieth century. Take two countries, for example. As Joseph R. Rosenbloom includes in his book *Conversion to Judaism: From the Biblical Period to the Present*, in Germany there were fourteen intermarriages for every one hundred marriages involving someone Jewish in 1901. Five years later, that number had increased to seventeen. In 1911, 22 percent of Jews intermarried. The number spiked in 1916 (perhaps because of the First World War) to 42 percent but declined again in 1921 to 25 percent. In 1927, six years before Hitler became chancellor of Germany, the intermarriage rate there was 35 percent.

The intermarriage rate in Switzerland in 1880 was 5.7 percent. In 1900, it was almost the same at 7 percent. By 1920 it was 13 percent.

These numbers are representative of post-Enlightenment Jews in Europe. Intemarriage, together with secularization and the much more serious situation of persecution ending with the Holocaust, resulted in a weak, dispirited, and declining Jewry.

There were antidotes. The United States was a powerful magnet for the poor, hungry victims of Russian persecution during pogroms, especially after the assassination of Czar Alexander II in 1881. The Land of Israel drew only a tiny fraction of those Jews who emigrated from Europe, but eventually it, too, would play a major role in Jewish life. For Europe, the center of Jewish life for a thousand years, the twilight of Jewish life was near.

It is sad irony to note that just as the numbers of Jews who were assimilating increased, as the Jews who intermarried doubled and doubled again, as the forces of deadly hatred solidified in Europe, the chances for Jews to increase their numbers and thus their communal strength through conversion diminished. By now, the Jews had absorbed the attitude the Jew haters wanted them to absorb, that conversion worked only one way—from Judaism to Christianity. That converts weren't really Jewish. That it wasn't a genuinely Jewish activity to seek converts. The long history of welcoming converts was forgotten.

Instead, there was hostility to conversion. In the 1870s, for example, Nathan Adler, then the chief rabbi for the British Empire, sent letters to Jewish leaders in Australia forbidding all proselytizing and saying that only converts he personally accepted would be allowed. Rabbi Adler was, in fact, opposed in principle to accepting any converts.

In Argentina in 1928, Rabbi Shaul Sirhon initiated a plan in the Syrian Jewish community, with the agreement of the Ashkenazi rabbis, to accept no conversions to Judaism.

The Reform movement, however, continued to keep the idea of conversion alive. Rabbi David Einhorn created a prayer book and included a special service for accepting converts.

There were conversion efforts in Europe. John Oswald Simon was a British attorney in the late nineteenth century. He proposed a Judaism shorn of its ritualistic elements but with its theological and moral parts intact.

But such sentiments, at odds with even much of nontraditional Judaism, were not widespread and were not widely accepted. The Jews of Europe, those who did not leave for America or the Land of Israel or some other place, such as in South America, seemed to be frozen in place emotionally. They could not, or did not want to, grasp the emerging anti-Semitism around them. Anti-Semitism, sometimes now spelled antisemitism, was a word coined in the late nineteenth century by Wilhelm Marr, German publicist, as a supposedly scientific term for hatred of the Jews, *Judenhass*. At the end of his life, Marr renounced his earlier views and begged the Jews to forgive him.

But he was only one man. Others sought no forgiveness. The march toward the Shoah continued. Europe's Jews didn't know it, but they were doomed.

There were other conversion stories involving group conversions to Judaism.

The Jews of San Nicandro are one of the most well-known groups. They are a small number of people who originally came from San Nicandro Garganico in Italy. Descended from fifteenth-century families, these Jews organized through the efforts of Donato Manduzio. He was a wounded World War I veteran who, based on his interpretation of biblical verses, converted to Judaism. His conclusions convinced some of his neighbors to follow him into Judaism. The San Nicandro Jews began to immigrate to Israel and essentially completed their journey in 1949. Some of the Jews, however, remained in Italy.

The Subbotniks, literally "Sabbatarians," are one of the most prominent of the Judaizing Christian sects. These groups generally believe it is necessary to follow the commandments Moses promulgated in the Hebrew Bible. Sometimes the word "Judaizers" is used negatively by Christians who believe Christianity completely superseded Judaism, and some Christians who follow some Hebrew customs therefore don't like the term.

The Subbotniks originated during Catherine II's reign near the end of the eighteenth century. As they formed, they practiced *brit milah*, were unitarian rather than trinitarian, accepted the Hebrew Bible exclusively, and observed the Sabbath on Saturday rather than Sunday. There were variations among the Subbotniks in these beliefs. A group of thousands of Subbotniks settled in Israel as part of the First Aliyah. During the era of the Holocaust, there were Subbotniks in areas of the Ukraine that the Nazis occupied. The Subbotniks were killed with Jews and were treated as Jews.

The Abayudaya, or "people of Judah," are a community of about two thousand in eastern Uganda that practices Judaism, such as keeping kosher as best they can and observing the Sabbath. Most of these people are recognized as Jewish by Reform and Conservative Jews.

The Abayudaya began with Semei Kakungulu, a military leader who originally became Christian when British missionaries converted him around 1880 under the purported pretense that he would then be appointed king of Bukedi and Bugisu, territories he had won in battle. The British, though, limited the size of the territory under his control and refused to make him king. In 1913, an angry Kakungulu became a follower of the Bamalaki sect, which believed in a mixed system focused on avoiding Western medicine and included both Jewish and Christian elements. Their belief system led to a struggle with the British over cattle that the Bamalaki refused to vaccinate.

Kakungulu's religious evolution wasn't finished. By 1919, he had come to believe only in the Hebrew Bible. He performed *brit milah* on himself and his sons and called his community Jewish. A man named "Yosef" arrived in 1920. He may have been a European, and he certainly knew about the Jewish calendar, including holidays. He stayed and taught the group for six months, not only teaching them the calendar but also introducing them to the idea of keeping kosher. Kakungulu set up a school to teach these new lessons.

Semei Kakungulu died in 1928 from tetanus. Samson Mugombe Israeli, a disciple, became the community's religious leader. The group separated itself as much as possible because of persecution. The number of Jews in the community was reduced to about three hundred.

In 1962, the Abayudaya met their second born Jew, an Israeli named Arye Oded, who told them about the Jewish state. Oded wrote about the group, until then unknown in the Jewish world.

In February 2002 a Conservative rabbi formally converted the then-existing four hundred members of the group. It is not surprising, therefore, that Gershom Sizomu, the Abayudays' current spiritual leader, enrolled at the Conservative-affiliated Ziegler

School of Rabbinic Studies. He was ordained as a rabbi in 2008 and returned to Uganda.

The Bnei Menashe, "Sons of Menasseh," are from Manipur and Mizoram, states in India. Several thousand of them, recognized as Jewish, have become Israeli immigrants. Their ancestors, called Chin, came from Burma originally following animism, a system that included ritual headhunting. They converted to Christianity in the nineteenth century. By tradition, they accept that their ancestor Manmasi was in fact Manasseh, Joseph's son.

They came to be called Bnei Menashe after an encounter with the dedicated Orthodox rabbi named Rabbi Eliyahu Avichail. He founded a group named Amishav and went in search of the ten lost tribes, investigating whether they might have a long-forgotten Jewish past. If he became satisfied that at one time they were Jewish, he helped convert them and bring them to Israel. That is what happened in the final decades of the twentieth century with Bnei Menashe. In 2005, Rabbi Shlomo Amar, one of Israel's two chief rabbis, accepted them as Jews, though he felt they were still obligated to undergo a formal conversion. India objected to Israelis coming to their country to perform the conversions, and so Israel stopped issuing visas. Some of the Bnei Menashe then went to places like Nepal to convert and seek help in resettling in Israel.

They received help from Michael Freund, founder of the organization Shavei Israel.

There were various other groups as well around the world, some of whom believed they came from Jewish ancestors.

But beginning at the end of the nineteenth century, the Jewish world shifted. It was in the United States, with its originally small Jewish population, one that swelled starting in the 1880s with the arrival of millions of immigrants, mostly from Eastern Europe, that Jewish life would find its new center.

And it was in the United States that the question of conversion to Judaism would continue to play out in very interesting ways.

6

THE GOLDEN LAND

Converts in the United States

Jewish life in the United States evolved only slowly. Until the end of the nineteenth century, Jews were in large part reluctant to cross the wide ocean and come to the new land. They were afraid that in that strange and wondrous place they would lose their traditions. Orthodox rabbis warned them that in the New World, good Jews couldn't keep kosher, that they would be forced to forsake the Sabbath. And so, while there were Jewish immigrants from Europe, they came in only small numbers until the assassination of the czar and the resulting legal restrictions and persecution joined the traditional reasons of poverty and lack of opportunity to create millions of immigrants. The reason this is important is that the small numbers of Jews meant that even with a relatively high intermarriage rate, the numbers were barely visible because the overall numbers were so low.

But while there were few Jews at first, from the beginning, they did make crucial contributions to American life, such as Haym Solomon's loans to help finance the American Revolution. The Jews also made a small number of converts. But the converts they sometimes made came from a troubling source.

As did the rest of the country, Jews struggled with the question of slavery. A few were slaveholders, and some of these slaves were converted to Judaism. Indeed, their descendants formed some Jewish congregations. This act of owning and converting slaves was only part of the racism then present. In some cases, the black slaves from Africa were not welcome as converts. For example, in the year 1820, "The Holy Congregation of the House of God," K.K. Beth Elohim in Charleston, South Carolina, adopted a new constitution for their synagogue. The constitution noted that the congregation would not encourage proselytes but also would not interfere with making them. The congregation wanted documentation about the legality of the conversion if new members wished to join. But, the constitution continued, "people of color" would not be accepted as converts.

The United States was still being influenced by the negative European Jewish attitudes toward converts. There was, for example, the decision in 1834 by Rabbi Akiba Eger the Younger, the Jewish religious leader in Posen, that Jews were not allowed to accept converts. The changes came, starting in England with Grace Aguilar, a novelist. She wrote a series of letters in 1842 titled *The Jewish Faith: Its Spiritual Consolation, Moral Guidance and Immortal Hope.* The letters, optimistic in tone, went back to the belief in Judaism's unique greatness as a religion and in the ultimate spiritual destiny of humanity to embrace the Jewish faith.

American Jews were still finding their footing. On September 15, 1825, for example, Mordecai Manuel Noah, a playwright, politician, and diplomat, tried to establish Ararat, a Jewish nation on Grand Island, near Buffalo, New York. The project achieved no success, as Jews rejected it. No one even recognized the radical nature of Noah's project. It is often seen only as a precursor of the Zionist movement, but in another sense it is a direct challenge to the model the United States offered as a home to the Jews. What

Noah envisioned was a separation of Jews, a way to maintain the faith and prevent the intermarriage that would one day explode in high numbers. Separation plans, then, seemed to run counter to the idea of conversion. We will examine converts in Israel in the next chapter, but it should be noted that there are various separation models that include a conversion component, such as when the Jewish entity (later a Jewish nation) sends out emissaries to seek converts or allows people to study in the entity in order to become Jewish. That is, Noah's plan, even if it had come to fruition, was not an end of the idea of welcoming converts. But Noah had misread the Jews around him.

American Jews, that is, didn't at all reject America, and at least some Americans didn't reject them. There was always some intermarriage, but, especially after the revolution of 1848 in Germany failed and brought many liberal refugees to American shores, non-Jewish Americans not only married Jews but, at least in some cases, wished to convert to Judaism. The newly emerging Jewish newspapers, especially *The Occident* (1843–1869) and *The American Israelite* (founded in 1854) trace the admission of converts to Jewish life as the Jewish population grew.

Undoubtedly Warder Cresson, whose story was mentioned in the introduction, is the most important American convert to Judaism in the nineteenth century. Because of that importance, Cresson's story is worth considering at some length.

Cresson was born in 1798 in Philadelphia to a Quaker family. Cresson grew up in a literary town, crackling with the stories and issues of the day. In particular, Cresson was a restless religious seeker. He first wrote an anti-Catholic pamphlet and then, dissatisfied with his birth religion, embarked on a series of spiritual explorations. One by one he examined different Protestant denominations, but he found none of them emotionally satisfying.

Isaac Leeser, the founding editor of the first general Jewish newspaper in America, *The Occident*, was one of the most influential Jews of the nineteenth century. Leeser met Cresson in 1840. The meeting prompted Cresson's interest in going to the Holy Land, though his original intent was to become a missionary. In 1844 Cresson went to Washington to apply to be the first American consul in Jerusalem. He was appointed on May 17. He left Philadelphia for England and then Jerusalem. Some politicians, though, thought Cresson mentally unsuited to represent the United States. They prevailed, and on June 22 his appointment was cancelled. Because he was already en route, Cresson did not learn of this withdrawal of the appointment. He reached Jerusalem in early fall, and in October he met the famed British author William Makepeace Thackeray. Cresson began to engage in missionary work, as he had desired, but as he got to know the Jews he was supposed to convert, he came to admire them, and he, more and more, objected to the use of what he called soul-snatching methods by the missionaries with whom he worked.

Cresson began exploring Judaism. He wrote to Mordecai Manuel Noah. And he began writing his book *The Key of David*, which explains his growing interest in the Jewish faith. It was on March 28, 1848, that Cresson formally converted and took the name Michael C. Boaz Israel. The Jews in Jerusalem certainly admired him and found him a curiosity. He was fervent, a passion that some would call madness and others a dazzling life energy. He claimed to see angels as he became a Jew. Warder Cresson had finally found a permanent spiritual home. He began to write articles about his experiences for *The Occident*. It was in those articles that Cresson publicly condemned the London Society for the Conversion of the Jews. The Jews in Jerusalem, particularly the farmers and the poor, especially admired Cresson. They began to think of him as someone who could work miracles; they asked him to pray for them when they got ill or found themselves in need.

On May 7, 1848, Cresson sailed for home, arriving there on September 20. He and his wife and family immediately began fighting over his religious activities. Only one of his sons accepted his choice to join the Jewish people. His family had him committed to a mental institution. A lower court accepted the incarceration, ruling that Warder Cresson was in fact insane. It was a crucial moment for religious freedom for Jews and indeed for all citizens of the United States. Cresson appealed the verdict. His trial opened on May 13, 1851. Almost one hundred witnesses were called in the trial. It was widely publicized. If someone could be found insane on the basis of his having converted to Judaism, then conversion would have no future in the United States. The trial itself, of course, made the phenomenon of conversion much more widely known than it previously had been. The question was whether or not the verdict would vindicate the convert.

The verdict was rendered shortly after noon on May 19. Warder Cresson was found not to be insane.

Cresson lived as a Jew in Philadelphia when he arrived back. He worshipped at Mikveh Israel, Leeser's synagogue. He published his book in 1851, got a divorce, and in 1852 returned to the Land of Israel. There he married Rachel Moleano and had two children: David Ben Zion, who died in 1863, and Abigail Ruth, who died in 1865. Herman Melville visited the Holy Land in 1857 for nineteen days and met Cresson, who became a model for a character in Melville's book-length poem *Clarel*.

Warder Cresson died in Jerusalem on October 27, 1860. He was buried on the Mount of Olives. Every Jewish business in Jerusalem closed on his burial date.

There are many other conversion stories from the nineteenth century in the United States. For example, David A. Magee was a Christian who lived in Sioux City, Iowa. It was there that he met Ada Hattenbach, whose father Godfrey was one of Sioux City's first Jewish settlers. Magee converted to Judaism and got married to Ada in 1876. After the marriage, Magee entered the meat-packing industry, and in 1897 he became mayor of the city. Throughout his life he took an active role in Jewish communal matters.

But it was especially after Warder Cresson, after conversion had been legally vindicated, nationally publicized, and embraced by a prominent citizen, that the United States was different. Conversion was now open for discussion, especially in the Reform movement.

That discussion, though, was mostly about conversion, not proselytism. American Jews, especially the Reform, welcomed genuine converts who on their own came to a rabbi and sought to join the Jewish people. In contrast to such an attitude, American Jews were much less supportive of proselytizing, of any active missionary effort to go out and seek converts. Passivity was still the norm when it came to conversion. Even within the general attitude of welcoming among some, however, there were still discussions and disputes about exactly how welcoming to be and how to show that welcoming attitude. At one end of the conversionary scale was the Reform rabbi Adolph Moses who sought to expand the mission idea of Judaism as far as possible. In an 1894 sermon, Rabbi Moses suggested that the word "Judaism" be changed to "Yahvism" to attract more Gentiles. As radical as this sounds, it should be remembered that "Judaism" was not the age-old term to refer to the religion of Jews; it was a post-Protestant, post-Enlightenment term. Of course, even with that, Jews had settled on "Judaism," had begun to think of Judaism as a religion (instead of an entire way of life), and were not about to change their name, especially to one so awkward as "Yahvism," and not just to attract converts.

As if Adolph Moses weren't radical enough, his ideas were taken even further by Sir Charles Waldston, an archaeologist and a writer who had been born with the surname Waldstein. In 1899, Waldston wrote a book titled *The Jewish Question and the Mission of the Jews*. He wanted the Unitarians, the theists, and other nontraditional Gentiles to enter the Jewish faith. After all, he argued, they, unlike traditional Christians, believed in a purer form of monothesism. Beyond that, Judaism had some unique elements to offer, especially a moral code and a great culture displayed over a long and fascinating history. To make Judaism more attractive for them, Waldston suggested that there be established a neo-Mosaic church, with all "Judaic" and "Hebraic" elements expunged. These he thought, in the language of the day, to be too racial. The traditional liturgy would be the basis of a revised liturgy offered in the vernacular languages of the various countries where this church was situated.

Converts to Judaism could be seen by Reform rabbis as a concrete example of their notion of mission and as a foretaste of their belief, traditional in its nature, that at the end of days people would freely embrace the Jewish faith. But in the United States especially, converts to Judaism provided another kind of solace and argument. There were in the United States many aggressive efforts by Christians to convert Jews. Sometimes such efforts were successful, and those promoting the conversion of Jews were quick to offer such converts as examples to other Jews. When rabbis found someone who converted to Judaism, such a person served as a perfect counterexample to the triumphalist notions of Christian missionaries. The converts to Judaism were a form of self-defense, almost a counterpunch to the conversionary efforts of the Christians. The converts to Judaism could show the weaknesses of the Christian argument. After all, if Christianity was so great, then how come these converts to Judaism had instead chosen to leave it and chosen to do so without any inducements, without fear of not going to heaven, without bribes?

It would be a false picture of nineteenth-century American Jews to assert that they were uniformly welcoming to converts. The attitudes, formed by isolation and persecution, had indeed hardened into the false belief that rejecting converts was somehow being genuinely Jewish. There were some in the Jewish community who said converts would weaken the Jewish people, diluting it, and therefore simultaneously weaken Judaism.

The opponents of conversion focused on several problems as they defined conversionary efforts. There had been cases in which the traditional rules of conversion had not been followed. Prior to 1840, for example, there were no ordained rabbis in the United States and so none to train converts, to oversee ritual requirements such as circumcision, *hatafat dam brit*, or immersion in the *mikveh*, no rabbis to serve as judges on a *bet din*. Therefore, it was argued, conversions to Judaism had been irregular, such as the conversions performed by the Jews in New York in the 1830s. The fact that there had been some irregularities with some conversions led to the argument that all conversions were to be suspect. (An obvious point should be inserted here. While opponents of conversion pointed out these abuses, they could just as easily have noted that rabbis were needed for other Jewish religious needs such as a divorce. The fact that conversion was the subject of complaint is an indication that deeper objections were held and that the abuses were at least partially just an excuse.)

Beyond not being able to accept converts as genuine Jews, the American Jewish community was worried about the reaction of the Christian community to the Jews accepting converts. The Jews were acutely conscious of themselves as belonging to a minority, a very new and fragile one in the United States. The focus of their concern again went back to the difference between conversion and missionizing. The Jews were afraid that accepting converts at all would be seen as accepting missionizing, that the

Jews were deliberately trying to lure Christians away from their religion. Even the fact that many of the conversions occurred because of an intermarriage did not relieve the Jewish fear that Christians would see converts to Judaism as proof positive of the Jews becoming missionaries. After all, Jews reasoned, Christians saw conversion through the lens of an active missionary effort. It was therefore feared that they wouldn't be able to distinguish between merely accepting converts who came on their own and actively undertaking a concerted effort to seek converts. Those rabbis, Isaac Wise prominently among them, who favored welcomed converts would note when they described someone or a group of people who had converted to Judaism that such conversions had aroused no animosity among the Christians in the area. Wise, in particular, was prescient in arguing that the United States was different, that here there was a variety of groups, that there was no state religion, and that the very pluralism of the nation meant that if one group welcomed converts then all should be able to do so.

Underlying these reasons to oppose conversion, naturally, were the inherited European attitudes that Jews didn't accept or seek converts. Those attitudes were changing, but they did so only very slowly. Wise's acute observation about what made the United States different didn't prove convincing to Jews, who still retained an understandable fear of their neighbors.

In a way, the story of conversion to Judaism in the United States hinges on the changes to these attitudes in the nineteenth century. There were new immigrants, younger people, those without deep religious ties, those willing to take chances, and those who wanted to let go of the old ways. More and more American Jews separated from the European model. They depended on themselves, on their perception that they were in a new land, and it was not going to be the same as the old one. They lived through the Civil War and fought to free the slaves. Surely, they saw in that a freeing of their own selves, a sense that their voyage across the waters had led them to a land where people were truly free to lead their own lives. Europe was getting farther away. Its language, its traditions, its attitudes held less and less power over American Jews.

It was the thoughtful Isaac Leeser who found the compromise when it came to conversion. Some Jews wanted to admit everyone who wished to become Jewish. Some Jews wanted to admit no one. Leeser suggested that the reasonable middle was to accept only those converts who were willing to adhere to the community's religious rules. Everyone, he suggested, should be willing to go along with that.

It is very difficult to translate these various arguments into reliable facts about what was happening in American Jewish religious life. One clear fact was the interrelationship between conversion and intermarriage. One study estimated that in the fifty years between 1790 and 1840 (that is, the year the first ordained rabbi arrived in the United States), there were 699 marriages involving someone born Jewish. Of these, 201 (or 28.7 percent) involved a marriage between someone born Jewish and someone born Gentile. Of the 201 intermarriages, the non-Jewish partner converted in twelve cases. It is interesting to speculate how these conversions occurred at a time of widespread Jewish hostility to conversion. Surely pressure by the Jewish partner's family must have played a major part. It is also unknowable how many additional people would have converted if a rabbi had been available to make the process more in keeping with tradition. Echoing the views of some who would come later, there were those in the Jewish community who saw in conversion a reasonable compromise. Jews could marry people they loved and still be part of the Jewish community, still raise Jewish children, still think of themselves as Jewish. No one at the time saw intermarriage as in any way positive, so conversion became an acceptable adjustment to reality.

One important way to chart the evolution (or devolution, depending on your point of view) of views on conversion is to examine what the various statements by the Reform movement included. After all, Einhorn, Wise, and the others, however important, were individual voices. The platforms offered by the movement were official statements, in principle at least coherent with the views of at least most members of the movement.

So let us take a look at these rabbinic pronouncements. The Conference of American Rabbis (that is, the official group of Reform rabbis) held a conference in Philadelphia from November 3 to November 6 in 1869. One of the resolutions passed at the conference focused on the mission of Israel. The resolution concluded that the Jewish people were not forced by God into their dispersal from the Land of Israel for their sins but rather in order to fulfill their divine historic purpose "to lead the nations to the true knowledge and worship of God."

The much more famous Pittsburgh conference was held from November 16 to 18, 1885. Isaac M. Wise served as the presiding officer of the conference, so it was inevitable that the mission of Israel would be discussed again. Reform Judaism's principles were laid out and indeed guided the movement for half a century. Regarding Israel's mission, the conference noted, "We hold that Judaism presents the highest conception of the God-idea as taught in our Holy Scriptures and developed and spirititualized by the Jewish teachers, in accordance with the moral and philosophical progress of their respective ages. We maintain that Judaism preserved and defended . . . this God-idea as the central religious truth for the human race."

The Columbus Platform of 1937 was the next statement. The very first statement of the platform, focusing on the nature of Judaism, included the notion: "Though growing out of Jewish life, its message is universal, aiming at the union and perfection of mankind under the sovereignty of God," and, further down in the statement, "We regard it as our historic task to cooperate with all men in the establishment of the kingdom of God, of universal brotherhood, Justice, truth and peace on earth. This is our Messianic goal." In regard to converts, the platform asserted, "The non-Jew who accepts our faith is welcomed as a full member of the Jewish community."

The Centenary Perspective adopted in 1976 is the first statement to appear after the Holocaust and the reestablishment of the state of Israel. It focuses on these and other contemporary events. It does not talk about the Jewish mission.

Finally, there was "A Statement of Principles for Reform Judaism," adopted in Pittsburgh in 1999. Here is a statement much more in keeping with traditional Judaism than with the early Reformers. The mission of the Jews is seen more in *tikkun olam*, repairing the world in partnership with God, than in making converts. But this statement was written after efforts by Rabbi Alexander Schindler, whose efforts are discussed below. Therefore, there was in this statement an explicit reference to converts: "We believe that we must not only open doors for those ready to enter our faith, but also to actively encourage those who are seeking a spiritual home to find it in Judaism."

This is quite a startling statement, for it explicitly endorses seeking, or "actively encouraging," people who wish to convert. Proselytizing has been officially reintroduced to Jewish life. Of course, there are limits to statements. Institutions have leaders who may or may not adhere to those statements. Words are not deeds. Still, it is remarkable that the Reform movement is officially reembracing the ancient tradition of actively seeking converts to Judaism.

All these statements, structured as guidelines to help the rabbinical members of the movement, had their limits. They were by their nature general statements. The details of Jewish life, though, were very far from general. They sometimes led to dispute.

One such dispute in the area of conversion for the Reform movement was whether circumcision was required for the conversion of a male candidate. Of course, for Orthodox and Conservative Judaism, no such argument was possible for circumcision (*brit milah*) was required, or the drawing of a drop of blood (*hatafat dam brit*) if the circumcision had already been performed. This requirement could not be waived.

As of 1892, the Reform movement accepts converts without *brit milah* (or another requirement, immersion in a *mikveh*). This decision was reached because such requirements are not mentioned as laws in the Torah and because there were minority opinions in the Talmud that circumcision was not a requirement for conversion. It should also be noted that Reform rabbis can, and in recent times more frequently do, suggest these traditional rituals be undertaken.

This decision to abrogate the traditional requirements had not been a decision taken without dispute. The Philadelphia Conference of 1869 was neutral on the subject, though most of the rabbis who attended believed it was not necessary to require *milah* for converts. The subject underwent discussion for several decades.

It was in 1890 that a man seeking to convert to Judaism without undergoing a *brit milah* approached Rabbi Henry Berkowitz in Kansas City and asked the rabbi to allow the conversion to proceed. Rabbi Berkowitz, evidently aware of the diversity of opinions, sought the views of some of the country's leading Reform rabbis. Three of the rabbis responded that a *brit milah* was obligatory. One of these was the eminent Moses Mielziner, a professor of Talmud at Hebrew Union College, the rabbinical seminary in Cincinnati. Ten rabbis responded by saying the applicant could be admitted without undergoing the *brit milah*. These included some of the most prominent names in the movement, including Isaac M. Wise, Kaufmann Kohler, Gustav Gottheil, and Emil G. Hirsch. Rabbi Berkowitz decided to follow the will of the majority, and he admitted the man who wished to join the Jewish people.

This case created controversy within the movement, enough controversy that the movement decided there had to be a resolution so that all rabbis would have a ruling to consider. In 1892 the Central Conference of American Rabbis ruled that a rabbi, with the agreement of two associates, could accept as Jewish any "honorable and intelligent person, without any initiatory rite." The rabbis, however, did wish to make sure that a potential convert sought to become Jewish freely, that the person have a good character, that the person be adequately trained in Judaism's essential faith and practices, and that the person provide sufficient evidence of a desire to worship one God, to live by God's laws, and "[t]o adhere in life and death to the sacred cause of Israel." Of course, the word "Israel" then referred to the Jewish people, not a nation.

Reform thinkers in particular focused on the notion of the mission of Israel. Kaufmann Kohler (1843–1926) was David Einhorn's son-in-law and Isaac M. Wise's successor as president of Hebrew Union College. Kohler's principal work was titled *Jewish Theology*. Part of his goal in the book was to assert that the idea of mission was inherent in all of Jewish thinking and was not a new invention by the Reform movement. He envisions Abraham as a wandering missionary. In a paper Kohler read before the Central Conference of American Rabbis in 1919, he made a startling assertion. In the wake of World War I, when faith in humanity's future was in doubt, Kohler suggested that if the Jewish people could fulfill its mission, that effort would benefit humanity—that this moment was when the Jewish mission was most needed.

The most compelling argument for a Jewish mission in the twentieth century came from Rabbi Leo Baeck (1873–1956), in part because of the rabbi's unique background and moral authority. On January 27, 1943, Baeck, almost seventy years old, was deported and sent to the Theresienstadt concentration camp. There he headed the council of elders. He organized lectures there. The camp was liberated in early May 1945. The Russian army handed over the camp guards to the Jewish inmates, who, understandably, sought vengeance against the guards. Rabbi Baeck argued with the inmates and eventually convinced them not to lose their own humanity by murdering the guards.

One day an American jeep arrived at the camp, and Major Patrick Dolan stepped out with orders to take Rabbi Baeck out of the camp and back to his relatives. But Baeck refused to leave, explaining that he was the rabbi of all those still stuck in the camp. Many of the inmates were at the point of death because of a typhus epidemic. He waited until all the remaining Jews were taken care of and then left the camp.

During the postwar years, Leo Baeck was president of the World Union for Progressive Judaism and lectured at the Reform movement's seminary in Cincinnati, Hebrew Union College, Jewish Institute of Religion. He was widely known for his extraordinary book *The Essence of Judaism*, in which he argued that Judaism would eventually become the religion of the entire world. In startling words he asserted, "Every presupposition and every aim of Judaism is directed towards the conversion of the world to itself."

His most famous speech about conversion came in the summer of 1949 at the union's sixth international conference. Dr. Baeck urged those present to see that the Jews were a people with a mission and that the mission was to offer Judaism to the world. He urged the conference attendees to understand that Judaism had a purpose, to designate people to carry out the purpose of winning converts, and to do it all openly. Interestingly, Baeck considered where the center of conversionary efforts should be established. Israel was a logical choice; after all, it was a miracle to reestablish a Jewish nation in the Land of Israel after two thousand years of dispersal, to revive the holy language of Hebrew, and to do so right after the worst tragedy in the history of the Jewish people, a people that had a history too often punctuated by tragedy.

But Baeck believed the center of these efforts should be in the United States. In words rarely spoken with such bluntness, Baeck said, "A place for missionaries must be established. We can no longer live without it. We would not see the signs of the times without seeing this. . . . The Jews of America can do it. They must do it."

There was, to put it mildly, resistance to this idea. Some rabbis thought any mission should be limited simply to those born Jewish. Some were, given history, afraid of the reaction of other religions, and some simply were not inclined to any new idea or new action. There was certainly no push on the rabbis from the Jewish laity. They, even more than the rabbis, were unwilling to reach out to seek converts.

And so, even in the Reform movement, the idea of actively encouraging converts persisted mostly as an intellectual idea but not as a program. That would not change for several decades.

It should not be supposed, however, that Reform rabbis were the sole proponents of encouraging conversion. A number of prominent Conservative rabbis also held this view. For example, Dr. Solomon Goldman wrote an experimental prayerbook in 1938. It was titled *Tefilot v'Shereem, Prayers and Songs*. Dr. Goldman wrote: "Judaism means to convert the world, not to convert itself."

Rabbi Robert Gordis was perhaps the most perceptive Conservative supporter of seeking converts. He wrote a chapter titled

"Missionary Activity and Religious Tolerance" in his book *Judaism for the Modern Age*. The theoretical work in this chapter was preparatory to a much more direct statement he made in an article titled "Has the Time Arrived for Jewish Missionaries?" that appeared in the March 1958 edition of *National Jewish Monthly*. Rabbi Gordis realized both the strengths and weaknesses of his suggestion. He therefore called for a discussion, one both full and frank, of such an effort. Interestingly, he suggested a pilot program to test his theory, and he wanted the program to be conducted in Japan, where, he noted, there had been considerable interest expressed in Judaism. In the United States, Dr. Gordis suggested that information centers be established. These centers would provide non-Jews with material about Judaism.

In 1979, the author contacted Dr. Gordis and asked whether he still believed in encouraging conversion. His response was: "I believe even more strongly than in the past in the importance of the right kind of educational and missionary effort to win accessions to our ranks."

Rabbi Seymour Siegel, who chaired the Committee on Jewish Law and Standards of the Rabbinical Assembly, the organization of Conservative rabbis, publicly endorsed converting Gentiles married to a Jewish partner. He was less sure about converting other Gentiles.

The Orthodox movement was split in its views regarding conversion. One faction permitted conversions of those who had intermarried or planned to and wished to convert in connection with such a romantic relationship. This group also encouraged Jews to accept as converts the children of an intermarriage with a Gentile mother. This group consisted of rabbis such as Zvi Hirsch Kalischer (who was also famous as a prominent forerunner of the Zionist movement), David Hoffmann, Marcus Horovitz, and the Imrei David, David Horowitz. But there was another group of Orthodox rabbis who were more stringent. It was this stringent approach that prevailed after World War II. Intermarriage had greatly increased, and this group believed that greater separation of Jews would reduce the intermarriage rate. With self-segregation, Jews and Gentiles could not meet and fall in love. Such a self-separation meant reduced contact for the Orthodox and so fewer opportunities to discuss Judaism and encounter someone interested in converting to Judaism. Additionally, the Orthodox found the changes in the Reform and Conservative movements to be distasteful, and as those movements became more open to converts, at least in theory, the Orthodox reacted against them and tightened restrictions. The Orthodox, that is, sought to present themselves as very different, especially from the Reform movement, and one way to do that was to make clear the difference in attitudes about potential converts.

It was because no movement actively sought converts that it was left to independent organizations to begin the effort.

David Horowitz, a Swedish-born journalist born in 1903, moved to the United States in 1943 after spending time in the Land of Israel and Poland, where he worked to rescue European Jews from the Nazis. Horowitz's wife was a convert, and in 1942 in Jerusalem, he helped to convert Boake Carter to Judaism. Carter was then a prominent radio news commentator. In the United States, he worked as a correspondent for the United Nations. He also founded the United Israel World Union in February 1944, the first incorporated Jewish organization to seek converts, or in the words of its founding document, "an international movement to disseminate the Decalogue Faith both within and beyond the confines of Jewry." The union published a bulletin and helped organize those who converted into a couple of small communities, one in West Olive, Michigan, and another in West Union-Wilbur, West Virginia. Horowitz was also the author of the book *Thirty-Three Candles.* He died in 2002.

Horowitz failed to find a wide audience among Jewish leaders, even some who welcomed the idea of attracting converts. The reason for this was, perhaps, his vision of Judaism, especially his notion "that the ten tribes of Israel, hitherto lost in identity, exist in the world today; that, during their long dispersion, both houses of Israel turned to Greco-Roman-Egyptian tenets which they substituted in the main, for the true inspired Mosaic code; that, if the great plan of Prophecy is to be fulfilled, a Union must now take place between the two separated houses of Israel whose breach has remained unhealed since the split of the Commonwealth after Solomon's reign." In urging potential converts to believe that they were descendants of the lost tribes, Horowitz, whatever his genuine sincerity and intentions, simply had gone away from traditional rabbinic views and so could not gather their support.

In the 1950s, renowned Orthodox leader Rabbi Joseph Soloveitchik joined together with other members of the Orthodox organization the Rabbinical Council of America to meet with Conservative leaders, especially the Talmudic expert Rabbi Saul Lieberman. The purpose of the group was to create a national *bet din*, or religious court, in the United States to deal with Orthodox and Conservative converts. The group wished to establish standards for personal issues of marriage and divorce. Their model was the Chief Rabbinate in Israel. The effort failed, in part because the Orthodox insisted that the Rabbinical Assembly (the organization of Conservative rabbis) expel some Conservative rabbis for what they had done prior to the formation of the *bet din*. The Rabbinical Assembly refused to do this. Some Orthodox rabbis were opposed to any cooperation with non-Orthodox rabbis, even ones who asserted that they followed all the rules of Jewish law.

It was in 1959 that Ben Maccabee, a refugee from Germany and an engineer living in Chicago, took note of an Israeli group. That group, the World Union for the Propagation of Judaism, had been established in Israel in 1956 by Dr. Israel Ben-Zeev, who headed Arab schools in Israel and served as a professor at the Orthodox-affiliated Bar-Ilan University. This group elicited very little attention, in part evidently because of the aim to convert Arabs in Israel as a way to deal with the internal national conflicts between the two peoples. As strange as such a notion might sound, it was that dynamic that had worked in ancient Israel when the people intermarried with the Children of Israel and adopted the Israelite religion. In this case, such an effort did not meet with widespread interest or approval.

But Ben Maccabee took note both of it and of interest and statements of support from various rabbis. He organized the Jewish Information Society. The society did gather much more widespread support by prominent Reform and Conservative rabbis and published a monthly journal between 1960 and 1969. The society did not succeed, and it did not do so for a familiar reason. While many rabbis supported this effort, there was no widespread support in the Jewish community. Without training in conversion's history and role in communal sustenance, the sort of training rabbis had, most Jews continued to hold long-believed myths about Judaism, that Jews had been a biologically consistent group throughout the ages, that conversion just wasn't Jewish, that converts couldn't really understand what it meant to be Jewish. These inaccuracies were not overcome through education, and they persisted making efforts to seek converts much more difficult. As Maccabee wrote in a personal note to Joseph R. Rosenbloom: "Promises of financial and literary contributions were reneged. . . . I am sorry to report that there are not even ten dedicated persons or foundations willing to make substantial contributions to the cause. . . . I nevertheless persisted spending thirteen years and substantial funds until illness stopped me." The depressing nature of this communication is revealing. There is adequate rabbinic support and inadequate financial and communal support. That condition persists.

In 1960 Rabbi Moshe M. Maggal, who had been born in Hungary, founded the National Jewish Information Service in Los Angeles. As Rabbi Maggal recalled, he was sitting in his study one day, conversing with God. At one point in their discussion, Rabbi Maggal asked God why the Jews suffered more than did the Gentiles. As he spoke, a book of commentary fell from the shelf, and Maggal read the page to which it opened. He recalled that as he read the passage he realized that Judaism was the best religion, and so he was determined to let others share in it. Then he began the NJIS. Maggal had served in the Israeli Defense Forces from 1948 to 1949. He immigrated to the United States in 1950. In 1954, he served as a technical advisor to Cecil B. DeMille during the filming of *The Ten Commandments.* Working with his wife, Rachel, Maggal saw the efforts of the NJIS as focusing on "reverting Jews to Judaism and proselytizing Gentiles to Judaism." Rabbi Maggal particularly sought to bring his message to American Gentiles who had no religion. The author was a vice president of this organization, which was only officially dissolved in 1992.

It suffered an identical fate as the other organizations, as did additional efforts. For example, Rabbi Allen S. Maller, a Reform rabbi, founded JOIN US (Jews United to Welcome Christians into the Family of ISRAEL) and the National Jewish Hospitality Committee, but the latter explicitly did not proselytize.

Lena Romanoff founded and directed the Jewish Converts and Interfaith Network, an organization for converts and all those in interfaith relationships. Romanoff provided counseling to those contemplating conversion as well as interfaith couples and their families. She organized many conferences and workshops on conversion, intermarriage, and interdating and lectured widely, including on numerous radio and television shows. In 1990, she wrote the extraordinary book *Your People, My People: Finding*

Acceptance and Fulfillment as a Jew by Choice. The book was influential in educating a new generation about conversion. She later produced a video titled *Who Am I?* about intermarriage from the perspective of a child of an intermarriage.

Lena Romanoff's wide experiences, her passion for helping people, and her psychological insights have inspired converts. She was widely known in Philadelphia for counseling interfaith couples, among her many activities. She has many valuable stories to tell. One of them involves white roses in December.

Starting in 1985, she began receiving a dozen long-stemmed pearly white roses every December 1. This might not seem particularly unusual, except that the white roses came from a dead man.

The man was named Joseph Steinman. He lived in Philadelphia, where he owned a chain of flower shops. One July day, Steinman called Lena. He wanted to discuss his son's marriage to a Gentile woman. Despite making the appointment, he didn't show up. Lena kept calling him, but he didn't respond. Six months went by. He called her again. In halting speech, he explained he had not been able to meet her because he had suffered a stroke. Steinman begged Lena to meet him at the hospital.

She went, and he explained the reason for his request for help. He wanted his daughter-in-law to convert to Judaism. He was aware that he was dying and wanted his only son to give him Jewish grandchildren. Lena knew she had to be careful. She explained that she didn't believe in pressuring people to convert and so her ability to persuade the woman might not have the result Mr. Steinman wanted.

He told her more of the story. He and his late wife had not attended the wedding and had not seen his son in three years. Their phone conversations were forced. Now, the sick man declared, the doctors had found stomach cancer. The doctors told him he probably had a few weeks to live.

The son and daughter-in-law were due to visit the next day, and so Lena promised she would be there as well. But the next day, his son arrived alone.

Technicians arrived to take Mr. Steinman for additional treatments, and so Lena and the son were alone. Lena, thinking the hospital room was not the best place to talk, suggested the two go to the coffee shop. There they spoke for three hours. His wife, he explained, didn't trust religion of any sort. Lena tried, without seeming success, to convince the son to have his wife visit.

The two returned to the hospital room with no solution to the problem.

A week or so later Mr. Steinman's condition worsened. Watching the man die, Lena knew she had to try again. She called the son and begged him to visit before his father died.

It was later that evening when the son and his wife both came into the hospital room. While father and son spoke, Lena led the wife outside. The wife turned to Lena and explained that she would not lie and say she was converting. It was unfair to want her to consider doing so. The wife asked what to do. Lena said, "Do what you can live with."

The wife went inside and spoke softly to Mr. Steinman, so that only he could hear. When the couple left, Lena learned what had happened. The wife had lied. She had told her dying father-in-law that she planned to convert. The couple continued to visit, watching the old man's life drain out of him. They were there, holding his hands, when he died.

Lena's feelings were torn. She had wanted the daughter-in-law to say she was converting, but the lie was troubling.

Mr. Steinman's estate began sending Lena the white roses.

The letter came with the roses on December 1, 1993. It was a letter from the daughter-in-law. She had converted to Judaism, and she wanted Lena to know.

This story is the human face of conversion and explains the urgency that Jewish professionals feel to solve conversion issues.

One of the most interesting efforts at conversion cooperation took place in Denver, Colorado, between 1978 and 1983. There a joint *bet din*, this time also including Reform rabbis, was formed. Its explicit purpose was to define and promote the same standards for those who wished to convert to Judaism under its auspices. During the five years of its existence, the *bet din* performed more than 750 conversions to Judaism. The *bet din* broke up in 1983 after the Reform movement had adopted its patrilineality resolution, which will be discussed below. The Orthodox and Conservative rabbis could not, they felt, continue participating with a clear conscience because the Reform movement had changed the definition of who is Jewish.

In 1992, the author of this book founded the Conversion to Judaism Resource Center as a project of the Suffolk Jewish Communal Planning Council. The center provided information and advice to people who were considering converting to Judaism and to those who did convert. Members of the advisory board of the Conversion to Judaism Resource Center included Rabbi Bradley Shavit Artson, Rabbi Rachel Cowan, Dr. Nan Fink Gefen, Dr. David Gordis, Rabbi Irving Greenberg, Yossi Klein Halevi, Dr. Edward Hoffman, Dr. Walter Jacob, Professor Julius Lester, Patti Moskovitz, Rabbi Barbara Penzner, Lena Romanoff, Susan Weidman Schneider, Rabbi Harold Schulweis, Rabbi Alan Silverstein, Rabbi Neal Weinberg, and Professor Zvi Zohar. Barbara Shair served as outreach director. The purpose of the center was not to effect conversion but simply to provide information about it. One principal way of doing that was to establish a website where direct contact with hundreds of rabbis from all movements was made available.

When the project ended, the website was taken over by Rabbi Celso Cukierkorn, who runs his own conversion program. His

brother, Rabbi Jacques Cukierkorn, runs Brit Braja Worldwide
Jewish Outreach, the world's first virtual synagogue in Spanish.
This organization is dedicated to helping the thousands of people
who wish to become Jewish or return to Judaism.

In 1995, Ash Gerecht founded the National Center to Encourage Judaism. The center publishes its occasional newsletter *The
Jewish Proclaimer*. The publication is sent to more than three
thousand synagogues and Jewish entities. It is a unique organization in that through grants it supports advertising in the non-
Jewish media about introduction to Judaism and conversion
classes. Additionally, the organization established the Gerecht
Family Institute for Outreach at Hebrew Union College, Jewish
Institute for Religion. This institute has educated hundreds of
rabbis, cantors, and Jewish professionals. Each year, many third-
year Hebrew Union College students attend one of three outreach weekends. There, the students learn about outreach issues
and get advice about how to build a welcoming community, how
to work with conversion students and their families, and the various and sometimes intricate legal and ritual matters regarding
conversion.

The late and widely respected scholar Dr. Gary A. Tobin left
his position as the director of Brandeis University's Maurice and
Marilyn Cohen Center for Modern Jewish Studies and founded
the San Francisco–based Institute for Jewish and Community Research. One of the institute's key initiatives, under the direction
of Diane Tobin, is Be'chol Lashon (In Every Tongue), which
"grows and strengthens the Jewish people through ethnic, cultural, and racial inclusiveness." Among its goals is to "[i]ncrease the
Jewish population by encouraging those who would like to be part
of the Jewish people."

In 1999, Tobin published *Opening the Gates: How Proactive
Conversion Can Revitalize the Jewish Community*. It was an important statement not only for its contents but also because its

author was one of the most respected Jewish social scientists in the country. In the book, Tobin made a blunt argument that Jews should build a community that attracted and welcomed converts.

At a May 1999 conference he organized at New York's Museum of Jewish Heritage, Tobin said the Jewish community could help itself if it reached out to the Gentile partners in interfaith relationships, their children, people who had Jewish ancestors, and Gentiles on a spiritual search. He noted that converts brought a particular enthusiasm for their new spiritual identity, an enthusiasm that inspired other Jews. Gary Tobin died in 2009 before he could implement his plans.

There were many other efforts by individuals and local synagogues and organizations. But none of these received sustained national attention or engendered a mass movement to encourage conversion. One of the reasons for this is that none of these efforts was part of the system that nurtures converts—that is, the synagogue system. Conversion efforts therefore had to go beyond individual effort and focus on the enthusiasm of the various rabbis and the willingness of congregational members to be receptive to converts.

That is why the most important step forward in the effort to encourage conversions came not just from an individual outside the organized religious establishment but at the very center of it. In December 1978, Rabbi Alexander Schindler, then president of the Union of American Hebrew Congregations, the central congregational body of Reform Judaism, put forth a proposal to welcome converts. It should also be noted that Rabbi Schindler had also chaired the Conference of Presidents of Major American Jewish Organizations. He was, that is, one of the religious leaders of American Jewry.

It is also worth considering Schindler's background. His father, a Yiddish poet in Poland who later moved to Germany, was a soldier in the Austrian army during the First World War. He was captured by the Soviets and sent to Siberia. There he met some Russian peasants who had decided to become Jewish. He told his son how loyal these people were and how they defended the Jewish community. Additionally, his father published a journal with two coeditors: Aimé Pallière, the French Catholic who had almost converted and felt very Jewish, and Nathan Birnbaum, the then-Orthodox man who had coined the term "Zionism." All three of these men had concluded that it was important to encourage converts to Judaism. Alexander Schindler's first article, written at fifteen, was about Pallière.

Rabbi Schindler reached the same conclusions as his father about conversion through religious study. He also received thousands of letters from Gentiles who had married Jews and wanted to convert.

Schindler had three main motives for making his proposal. The first motive was defensive. The Jewish population, he knew, was declining. The birth rate was low. Second, he wanted to spur discussion within the Jewish community about conversion. His third motivation was that he believed Judaism had great spiritual content to offer the world.

He proposed the radical idea of converting "the unchurched" to Judaism. He wanted to start with those married to Jews but expand that notion to include anyone. He asserted that millions of Americans sought truth. He advocated starting a new commission to undertake this outreach program.

Following his address, the board of trustees adopted a resolution creating the Reform movement's outreach efforts. The story of his speech was on the front page of the *New York Times*. Alexander Schindler had put conversion front and center in Jewish life.

His efforts had lasting effects on the Reform movement. These will be discussed below. But his efforts became muddied for two reasons. The first of those reasons was a category confusion be-

tween making an active effort to win converts and general outreach efforts more broadly conceived. "Outreach" became a
catch-all term to refer to efforts to welcome intermarried couples,
gay Jews, people of color, people with disabilities, and so on. The
idea of outreach was fulfilled by welcoming those in a congregation who were intermarried. A vast majority of them were not
interested in converting. Some born Jews were offended that
their born-Gentile spouse would be asked to convert. (Rarely
were the born-Gentile spouses offended.) Soon the other efforts
to be welcoming, worthwhile though they were, directly inter-
fered with efforts to seek converts. Practical judgments were
made. On the one hand, wealthy congregants sometimes chafed
at even a discussion of conversion, and no one complained about
helping intermarried members of a congregation. Reform congregations that might have followed Schindler's plan instead found
themselves taking the understandably easier route of not talking
about conversion so as not to offend anyone. Conversion, to be
fair, was still there as an option, as we'll see, but it was not the sort
of effort Schindler had originally envisioned.

The second reason that Schindler's efforts didn't have profound consequences was that a year later, in December 1979, he
followed up with another major proposal, one that the offspring
of any mixed marriage would be presumed Jewish so long as they
made appropriate and timely acts, both public and formal, to
indicate their identification with Judaism and the Jewish people.
That is, the child of a Jewish father and non-Jewish mother would
be considered Jewish if the child were brought up exclusively as
Jewish and identified as a member of the Jewish people. Judaism
had traditionally, but not always, operated on the matrilineal principle, that any child of a Jewish mother was Jewish but a child of a
non-Jewish mother would have to convert formally to be considered Jewish.

What Schindler and his supporters failed to recognize, or recognized and chose to ignore, was that the patrilineality principle unintentionally undercut the Reform movement's historical initiative to seek converts. Why, after all, should a prospective female convert undertake the study, preparation, and commitment necessary for such a major step when her children would be presumed Jewish anyway? Almost a quarter of converts indicated that the most important reason for the conversion was to have a unified religious home. Having Jewish children evidently satisfied those people. Indeed, after the resolution passed, the rates of intermarriage increased and the rates of conversion dropped. In fairness, this might be coincidental. Intermarriage became more socially acceptable.

The Conservative movement, meanwhile, undertook various projects as well, under different names.

In 1991, the United Synagogue of Conservative Judaism created the Commission on the Prevention of Intermarriage. Among its efforts, the commission established a toll-free number where interested people could get information about conversion. Rabbi Alan Silverstein wrote several key pamphlets and books about intermarriage and conversion. In 1995, the Rabbinical Assembly established the Committee on Giyyur, and the RA and United Synagogue in 1996 established the Joint Commission on Responding to Intermarriage.

The author was a member of all these committees (ex-officio of the RA's) and wrote various books about conversion (see the references). He interviewed Rabbi Schindler about the conversion proposal a week before the patrilineal speech.

All of these efforts had limited success. There was certainly an increase in conversions. There were many more stories. Conversion was an idea that had come out of hiding. In that sense, conversion efforts have had a distinct but limited success.

Such efforts continue.

The Reform movement provides information about conversion on its official website: http://www.reformjudaism.org/practice/ lifecycle-and-rituals/conversion.

Additionally, the Reform movement has two introductory classes. The first is a three-session class for beginners, titled "A Taste of Judaism . . . Are You Curious?" at http://www. reformjudaism.org/learning/judaism-classes/taste-judaism. The website describes the class this way: "Enjoy three weekly classes on the modern Jewish take on spirituality, values, and community. Our classes are dynamic and interactive; our teachers are accessible, fun, and can answer any and all of your questions."

The second Reform class is a sixteen- to twenty-week course for, among others, those who wish to convert. The link is http://www.reformjudaism.org/learning/judaism-classes/intro-judaism. The website describes the class this way: "URJ Introduction to Judaism is a course offered in partnership between the Union for Reform Judaism and local Reform congregations for anyone interested in exploring Judaism—singles, interfaith couples, those considering conversion and Jews looking for adult-level basics. This class introduces the fundamentals of Jewish thought and practice in sixteen to twenty weeks. Topics include Jewish holidays and life cycle events, theology and prayer, Israel, history and Hebrew."

The Conservative movement also has current efforts to welcome converts. The official website of the movement has a page titled "Considering Conversion to Judaism?" at http://www.uscj. org/JewishLivingandLearning/ApproachingtheIntermarried/ AboutConversiontoJudaism.aspx.

The American Jewish University, affiliated with the Conservative movement, has an Introduction to Judaism program in various southern California locations, including Los Angeles. See http://intro.aju.edu/. The Miller Introduction to Judaism program is perhaps the largest program preparing people for conversion in

North America; it is certainly among the largest. It is therefore worth examining its curriculum, available at its website.

> Our engaging, university-level course is offered over eighteen sessions and includes Hebrew language instruction for every level. Classes are interactive and discussion based, with many opportunities for questions and for experiential learning in and out of the classroom.
>
> Complete the course at your own pace—accelerated options available.
>
> Class One: Beginnings: From Creation to the Edge of the Wilderness
>
> Class Two: The World of the Bible
>
> Class Three: Heart of Many Rooms: Understanding Jewish Diversity
>
> Class Four: Holy Days: The Wheel of the Jewish Year
>
> Class Five: Shabbat: Palace in Time
>
> Class Six: When Do I Bow? And Other Questions about Jewish Prayer
>
> Class Seven: Passover: The Jewish Master Story
>
> Class Eight: God: Encountering the Holy
>
> Class Nine: Talmud: Argument for the Sake of Heaven
>
> Class Ten: Starting Over: The High Holy Days
>
> Class Eleven: Kashrut: The Original Soul Food
>
> Class Twelve: Philosophers, Poets, and Mystics: The Jewish Middle Ages
>
> Class Thirteen: Marriage, Love & Kosher Sex
>
> Class Fourteen: From Birth to B'nai Mitzvah: Raising a Mensch
>
> Class Fifteen: A Time to Mourn: Traditions for Death, Grief, & Healing
>
> Class Sixteen: Out of the Darkness: Stories from the Holocaust
>
> Class Seventeen: Israel: Dreaming of Deliverance
>
> Class Eighteen: The Jewish Mission to Heal the World

There is also a conversion program sponsored by the Rabbinical Assembly at various sites in New York City: http://www.ExploringJudaism.org.

The Orthodox movement is splintered in various ways. There is therefore no single official website to represent the entire movement. The Rabbinical Council of America comes the closest. It has information about its conversion program on its official website: http://www.judaismconversion.org/.

The Reconstructionist movement's conversion information can be found at http://www.therra.org/RRA%202009%20Guidelines %20on%20Giyyur.pdf.

Finally, there are many additional excellent conversion programs. One of the largest and best known is at the 92nd Street Y in New York: http://www.92y.org/Uptown/Bronfman-Center-for-Jewish-Life/Programs-Resources/Derekh-Torah.aspx.

There are many additional sites, including blogs, mentioned with links in the references at the end of the book.

There are many individuals, some famous but most not, who have converted to Judaism in the United States and elsewhere in contemporary times. A fuller list can be found on Wikipedia's list of converts to Judaism: http://en.wikipedia.org/wiki/List_of_ converts_to_judaism.

Here are some of the people who have converted to Judaism:

Carroll Baker

Carroll Baker is an American actress born in 1931. She is perhaps most famous for the lead role in the 1956 Elia Kazan film *Baby Doll*. She got an Oscar nomination for the film, which made good use of her beauty, drawl, and the striking brashness of her screen personality, used in several of her films. Some of her other films included *Giant* (1956) with James Dean and Elizabeth Taylor; *But Not for Me* (1959), co-starring Clark Gable; and various westerns.

Baker was married three times. Jack Garfein was her second husband. Garfein was born in 1930 in what is now the Ukraine. He was imprisoned in Auschwitz and immigrated to the United

States at the end of the war. In New York, he became part of the Actors Studio, and it was there that he met and in 1955 married another student, Carroll Baker. Baker had been raised as a Catholic but converted to Judaism in the context of her relationship with Garfein, who went on to be a film and theater director and an acting teacher. The couple had a daughter and a son before divorcing in 1969.

Polly Bergen

Polly Bergen, born in 1930, is an American actress. She has additional career paths as a singer, businesswoman, and television host. Her most famous film was *Cape Fear* (1962). Bergen was awarded an Emmy for portraying the singer Helen Morgan. She was a regular panelist on the CBS TV game show *To Tell the Truth* (1956–68).

She married Freddie Fields, a talent agent and film producer. Born a Southern Baptist, she converted to Judaism after her marriage to Fields.

May Britt

May Britt is a Swedish actress. She met the African American entertainer Sammy Davis Jr. in 1959, and the two wed on November 13, 1960, a few days after the Kennedy-Nixon election. Indeed, there was a widely circulated story at the time that both John and Robert Kennedy asked Frank Sinatra to convince Davis to delay the wedding until after the election because of the racial controversy. Thirty-one states did not then allow interracial marriages. Such laws were ruled unconstitutional in 1967. Davis, to be discussed below, had famously converted to Judaism, and May Britt followed suit in October 1960 in conjunction with the Jewish holiday of Succot. Rabbi William Kramer performed their wedding ceremony.

Yisrael Campbell

Yisrael Campbell, born in Philadelphia, is a comedian living in Israel. He was brought up a Catholic, even with a nun as an aunt. Campbell is famous for having three conversions to Judaism, first with a Reform rabbi, then with a Conservative one, and, finally, with an Orthodox rabbi. It was while visiting Israel for four months in 2000 that he concluded he needed that third conversion. He is the central focus of the play and 2008 film *Circumcise Me*.

Kate Capshaw

Kate Capshaw, born in 1953, is an American actress. It was while she was filming *Indiana Jones and the Temple of Doom* (1984) that she met the film's director, Steven Spielberg. Born an Episcopalian, Capshaw converted to Judaism prior to her marriage to Spielberg on October 12, 1991. The two had a civil and an Orthodox wedding ceremony.

Abraham Carmel

Carmel was a Roman Catholic priest who practiced his vocation with great devotion for seven years. Slowly, however, theological doubts entered his mind, and he found he could no longer consider Jesus divine. He felt adrift and began what amounted to a desperate search for a solution to his problem. One day he found himself reading Joseph Klausner's provocative and scholarly book *From Jesus to Paul*. One of the book's principal arguments was that Jesus was a Jewish teacher, the literal meaning of the word "rabbi," whose teachings, all of which had a foundation in Judaism, were transformed by the missionary Paul into a dogmatic system with a large organization to promote what amounted to the ending of Jewish law and a compromise with pagan beliefs. Klausner had argued that Jesus had remained Jewish throughout his entire life and never intended to found a new religion. For his part, Carmel was stunned as he turned the pages. He suddenly realized that he believed the basic idea that it had been Paul rather than Jesus who had been the true founder of Christianity. Carmel was relieved in a certain way because he had found a valuable way to understand his own religious roots. This new understanding began an intense reevaluation of all his spiritual beliefs. Step by step, he found no justification for not following Jesus's original religion: Judaism. He converted to Judaism and for a time moved to Israel, only returning to the United States for health reasons. Back in the United States, he became a prominent Jewish educator. He wrote a fascinating book about his experiences. The book is titled *So Strange My Path*. He died at age seventy in 2009.

William Holmes Crosby Jr.

Crosby (1914–2005) was a physician considered as one of the founders of modern hematology.

Sammy Davis Jr.

Sammy Davis Jr. was one of the most famous entertainers in the United States during his heyday. He was part of the "Rat Pack" along with Frank Sinatra, Dean Martin, Joey Bishop, and others who were friends and fellow performers. It was the comedian Eddie Cantor who first interested Davis in Judaism. Davis was waiting to appear on Cantor's television program when he noticed a *mezuzah*-like ornament in the dressing room. He mentioned his admiration of the object, and Cantor gave it to him. Davis wore it every day until one day in 1954, when he replaced it. Later that day he had an automobile accident that caused him to lose an eye.

Davis was in the hospital convalescing. A rabbi was one of the visitors who came to wish him well. Davis started asking the rabbi about Judaism, and the rabbi answered and gave Davis some books to read. Once he recovered from the accident, Davis began to speak to various rabbis. He had a lot of questions. Continuing to study, Davis concluded several months later that he wanted to convert to Judaism.

As an African American, Davis was subject to a considerable amount of discrimination. While his parents did not object to his conversion, a number of friends warned him against it. Some feared that the public would see the conversion as some sort of publicity stunt.

But Davis was positive. Judaism gave him some sort of inner strength that he needed. He went through with the conversion.

Davis's new faith in Judaism confronted a hurdle soon after he embraced the Jewish faith. He was then filming *Porgy and Bess* (1959). Filming was supposed to take place on Yom Kippur, and Davis told the director that his faith forbade him from filming on the most sacred Jewish holy day, the Day of Atonement. The director was not happy and immediately called the producer, Samuel Goldwyn, who was known for his tough, no-nonsense style. Goldwyn immediately called Davis. The entertainer said he could not in good conscience as a believing Jew work on Yom Kippur. Goldwyn was silent for a moment, and then, in a quiet voice, Goldwyn blessed Davis and hung up.

There was no production of *Porgy and Bess* on Yom Kippur, a choice that cost Goldwyn $30,000. Later, Davis married the white, Swedish actress May Britt. He died of throat cancer in 1990.

Capers Funnye

Rabbi Capers Funnye is himself African American and heads Beth Shalom B'nai Zaken Ethiopian Hebrew Congregation in Chicago. There are two hundred members of the congregation, most of whom are African American. Funnye is Michelle Obama's first cousin, once removed. He was raised in the Methodist faith, explored other alternatives, and eventually found his way to Judaism.

Jamaica Kincaid

Kincaid is a prominent novelist born in Antigua in 1949. In 1979, she married Allen Shawn, a professor at Bennington College and the son of William Shawn, the well-known editor of the *New Yorker*. The actor Wallace Shawn was her brother-in-law. At some point, she chose to convert to Judaism. She and Shawn divorced in 2002.

Kincaid had known William Shawn, who served as a writing tutor of sorts and hired her as a staff writer, a position she held for two decades. She left the *New Yorker* in 1996 after the new editor, Tina Brown, decided that the comedian and actress Roseanne Barr would be chosen as a representative of feminism to serve as a guest editor for an issue of the magazine. Kincaid resented Brown's focus on celebrity rather than continuing the magazine's more distinctly literary tradition.

Mathilde Krim

Mathilde Krim, born in Italy in 1926, founded amfAR, which is devoted to AIDS research. Prior to that she participated in the Irgun, the Jewish movement important in achieving Israel's independence. She married Arthur Krim, an attorney and founder of Orion Pictures, in 1958 and converted to Judaism. Later, in 1962, he joined Sloan-Kettering Institute for Cancer Research.

Anne Meara

Anne Meara was born in 1929. She and her husband, Jerry Stiller, formed a popular comedy team known as Stiller and Meara. The two are the parents of Ben Stiller, the actor and comedian, and actress Amy Stiller. Meara converted to Judaism six years after she married Jerry Stiller and has long noted that the conversion was not because of the marriage but because she was deeply attracted to Judaism.

Marilyn Monroe

The famed glamorous actress Marilyn Monroe met the well-known playwright Arthur Miller at a Los Angeles party in 1951—that is, before she became truly famous. Besides Miller, Monroe came in contact with a lot of prominent Jews, perhaps especially Lee Strasberg, her acting coach, and his actress daughter, Susan.

Miller and Monroe married in a civil ceremony in late June 1956. By July 1, Marilyn had completed a conversion to Judaism, and so the couple were remarried, this time in a Jewish ceremony conducted by Rabbi Robert Goldburg, a Reform rabbi, at Congregation Mishkan Israel in New Haven, Connecticut. They had tried to keep the religious ceremony a secret by having photographers focus on the civil ceremony.

Marilyn's interest in Judaism was not at her husband's request. She had been brought up in a dysfunctional fundamentalist Protestant home. She found the Jews she met to be in sharp contrast to the people she had grown up with, and she began to read about great Jews in history. She particularly admired Albert Einstein. Additionally, in reaction to the nature of her religious upbringing, she found Judaism more rational. She liked its emphasis on the ethical, especially the Jewish emphasis on the family. She saw Jews as history's underdogs and identified with them in that way. Finally, she wanted to show Miller and his parents that she was loyal to them and saw conversion as the best route to do that.

Marilyn studied with Rabbi Goldburg for her conversion, meeting him numerous times to discuss the books he had given her to read.

Marilyn evidently took the conversion seriously. While Miller was not a religiously observant person, the family celebrated Hanukkah and Passover. The marriage was a troubled one, and the couple divorced in January 1961. However, Marilyn explicitly told Rabbi Goldburg that she had no plans at all to renounce her conversion to Judaism. She died in August 1962.

Daniel Silva

Daniel Silva, born in 1960, is an author of thriller and espionage novels, most prominently the novels about Israeli agent and art restorer Gabriel Allon. In 2009, Silva was appointed to the Memorial Council of the United States Holocaust Memorial Museum. Born Catholic, Silva converted to Judaism when he was an adult.

Ivanka Trump

Ivanka Trump, born in 1981, is the executive vice president of development and acquisitions at the Trump Organization, headed by her father, the flamboyant businessman Donald Trump.

She converted to Judaism in July 2009 and in October of that year married Jared Kushner, a businessman.

Devorah Wigoder

Born Jane Frances MacDwyer, Devorah Wigoder fell in love with Geoffrey Wigoder, a learned rabbi and scholar, and wished to marry him. Wigoder was very prominent in the Conservative movement, but while he was very proud to marry a woman who sincerely wished to convert independent of their romantic relationship, other people questioned whether so important a rabbi should marry a convert, in effect giving permission to others to do the same. Having taken a Hebrew name, Devorah went to see various well-known faculty members at the Conservative flagship institution of higher learning, the Jewish Theological Seminary. She sought their approval so as to avert future criticism of the marriage. She wanted, that is, to protect both her husband's reputation and the marriage itself. Rabbi Abraham Joshua Heschel, one of the most significant Jewish theologians of the century, gave his approval. Then Devorah approached the most renowned Talmudic scholar at the institution. She decided that Professor Saul Lieberman would provide the final test about whether or not the marriage would be approved.

One evening, after all the classes had been completed, Devorah went to Professor Lieberman's office door. She had decided to dress completely in black to symbolize how solemn she thought the moment.

Lieberman opened the door. She stared at his startling blue eyes and greeted him in Hebrew, only sometime later realizing she had used the feminine forms. Lieberman responded in French. She told him she sought a single advantage over him and asked that they converse in English. He agreed.

Devorah began the conversation by discussing how close she felt to the Talmud, how much she loved the Hebrew language, especially the Hebrew letters. She offered some views about the alphabet. Lieberman asked her whether she had read any books about the Hebrew alphabet. She said she hadn't. He said he liked that. It would be better, he suggested, if she kept studying and one day wrote her own book about the alphabet.

The two spoke, and then Lieberman told Devorah a story about a very learned rabbi who one day met a shepherd. The curious rabbi asked the shepherd how he prayed. The shepherd was embarrassed because he could not read Hebrew, so he quickly muttered the truth, that he prayed he loved God and that if God had sheep the shepherd would take care of them for nothing. The rabbi was shocked because the shepherd did not follow the required content and order of prayers as laid out in the prayer book. The rabbi immediately began teaching the shepherd about the correct prayers to say. The rabbi, though, continued to think about the shepherd, impressed by the closeness to God that the shepherd felt when he prayed. Then the rabbi returned and told the shepherd to forget what the rabbi had taught him, that the shepherd's natural words with God were much better.

Then Lieberman said he would write a letter to Geoffrey Wigoder's father, who opposed the marriage, telling him that Devorah was a genuine convert.

Devorah and Geoffrey eventually married and moved to Israel.

Madonna

Madonna is not a formal convert to Judaism but is included here because she is often thought to be one. The confusion arises because Madonna very vocally follows a modern version of Kabbalah, an ancient Jewish mystical tradition. She wears as a symbol of her beliefs a red string around her left wrist. Followers believe the string will provide protection from the *ayin hara*, the "evil eye."

Conversion is so complex a phenomenon, so filled with sometimes strange and fascinating stories. Sometimes, for example, family secrets emerge. Consider the case of the young woman who wrote the author about this story. The woman approached her family. She had met a Jewish man and wanted to convert and then marry him. Her parents were a bit troubled but sternly told her not to tell her grandmother, who was too religious to accept such a step. The young woman, though, loved her grandmother and felt she needed to be honest. And so, one day, she approached the grandmother and told her of the decision to embrace the Jewish faith. The grandmother heard the story and jumped out of her chair, headed quickly for her bedroom. The young woman heard the loud sobs through the door. Unhappy that she had so upset her grandmother, the young woman knocked and went inside, telling her grandmother that she was sorry for causing her such pain. The grandmother brought the woman close to her and revealed that she had been born Jewish but had hidden that fact for almost her entire life since she had gotten married. She had never even told the young woman's parents. The grandmother looked at her granddaughter and said nothing could make her as happy as the act of her becoming Jewish.

Sometimes a conversion to Judaism had its origins in anti-Semitism. Hate can require redemption, and once in a while it does. There are, for example, a variety of conversion stories related to the Holocaust. Haviva Strugazow was close to her Jewish father, who had survived the Holocaust. Haviva wanted to maintain the link to the Jewish past. Allyson D. Nesseler's father had been in the division that liberated Auschwitz, so for her, the Holocaust was a vivid part of the stories she heard in her childhood. Sometimes, though, the motives come from a darker place. Dr. Gilya Gerda Schmidt saw in conversion the only way to react to what she saw as the crimes committed by her parents' and grandparents' generations. She wanted to make up for some of the six million Jews lost.

And then there are the anti-Semites themselves. Earlier there was a discussion of a Nazi who became a Jew. There are also more home-grown haters of Jews. Consider, for example, the strange case of Larry Trapp, at one time the grand dragon of the Nebraska Ku Klux Klan. In June 1991, Trapp, acting on his Klan beliefs, called Michael Weisser, who was a cantor at a Reform congregation in Lincoln. It was an unpleasant, threatening call. Cantor Weisser phoned the police, who installed a tap on the phone. Only a few days later, Weisser got a package filled with hate literature from the Klan, the Nazis, and the Aryan Nations. Weisser immediately thought of Larry Trapp, who was infamous in the area for sending such materials. Although only in his forties, Trapp was blind and, because of his diabetes, confined to a wheelchair.

Weisser discussed the situation with his wife, who made a startling suggestion. She thought that her husband should speak with Trapp, not in a hostile, confrontational way but in a kinder manner. Weisser got Trapp's number. The phone's answering message was filled with vile hate against blacks and Jews. Undaunted, Weisser left a message telling Trapp that one day he would have to answer to God, and so he should think about what he was doing.

Weisser made a follow-up call to Trapp in a few weeks, reminding him that the Nazis hated people with physical handicaps. Weisser would not quit. He kept making the calls.

Trapp finally did pick up the phone, saying Weisser was harassing him and threatening to have the cantor arrested.

Weisser shocked Trapp with the response, saying he thought Trapp might need a lift to the grocery store.

The article in the paper came two weeks later. Larry Trapp had been sponsoring an anti-Semitic cable television show, but now he pulled it off the air. The article suggested Trapp was rethinking his racist views.

Weisser immediately called, wanting to find out whether the article was accurate. Trapp did not want to talk about it then. But the time came. Trapp called the cantor and said it was time to get away from what he had been doing. He asked for help.

Weisser and his wife visited Trapp. The cantor shook his hand. Trapp cried. He took off two rings that had swastikas, asking Weisser to get rid of them. They spoke for several hours. The Weissers left, and with them they took cartons of Nazi flags, hate-filled literature, and, tellingly, Trapp's Ku Klux Klan robes. Larry Trapp was cleaning his life.

Trapp apologized for all he had done. In early 1992, Trapp announced that he was studying Judaism. Eventually his illness made him unable to take care of himself. The Weissers invited him to move in with them, where Mrs. Weisser took care of him after giving up her job. Trapp completed his conversion to Judaism in June 1992. He died at age forty-three the following September. Larry Trapp, former Klan leader, former Nazi sympathizer, was buried in a Jewish cemetery.

Of course, beyond all these people, many thousands of other people have also chosen to embrace Judaism. Individually, their stories are dramatic snapshots of a life in search of meaning and love. Collectively, they make a significant contribution to contemporary American Jewish life.

Besides converts in the United States, the question of joining the Jewish people is nowhere more important than it is in Israel, where in many ways the future of the Jewish people will be played out, where the arguments are the loudest and the spiritual stakes are the highest.

7

THE CALL OF ZION
Converts in Israel

Conversion in Israel is a special case for various reasons. Most significantly, Jewish life in Israel is very different from Jewish life in the United States because in Israel there are chief rabbis and religious courts and because Orthodox Judaism dominates the religious landscape. Reform and Conservative rabbis have had to fight long battles to get any recognition.

It should also be noted that the legal status of converts is particularly fluid, and so it is impossible to provide here any definite statement about the status of converts in Israel. Instead, there is general information provided.

It might be concluded that the only questions involving Israel and converts are theological or legal ones since Zionism as an ideology seems to focus only on one group of people, the Jews, and so therefore dismiss Gentiles who might at some point be attracted to Judaism. Zionism might falsely be considered narrow and particularistic as opposed to more universal interpretations of Judaism or other worldviews, such as socialism, which claimed to explain not only the Jewish situation but the entirety of the human condition and to offer a solution to the problem of organizing humans into society.

This, though, is a narrow interpretation of Zionism. The Zionist theoreticians transformed the path to a just world from the more traditional Jewish notion of a fundamental relationship between God and the Jews to a social relationship between the Jews and the rest of humanity.

One interpretation of this Zionist plan to redeem humanity was to create a model state, a Jewish state. Zionists realized the state would not be perfect, but it would be an example of people struggling to be moral and honest, a state unlike other states, one grounded in Judaism. This Jewish state would focus on the ethical monotheistic roots of Judaism and in doing so provide a model by which other nations could shape themselves.

But as soon as this idea was propounded, there was an obvious question. If Zionism wished to create a model state, how would it transmit its redemptive message? The Zionist mechanism for universal redemption was to seek converts. Obviously, it is not possible to effect the conversion of all people, but the vision was to convert enough people in enough nations to the foundational idea of Judaism, ethical monotheism, that the world would turn from its current condition into a place worthy of God having created the world. Proselytizing, that is, is inherent in Zionist theory. While Israel has been forced to focus on its security, there are hints of a more universal mission in its actions, and once Israel is at peace, it can turn from the vital but limiting issues of survival to the larger questions of its historic efforts to redeem humanity.

Israel's creation in 1948 resulted (and continues to result) in a tumultuous legal struggle among those who have different ideas of who can convert to Judaism, the requirements for conversion, and who can perform conversions.

In Israel, the issue of conversion is wrapped up in what is more widely defined as the "Who is a Jew?" issue, and many of the attempts to solve issues of conversion have been in the context of defining what exactly it means to be Jewish in Israel. There is a specific focus here, of course, on matters that involve conversion, but the wider issue could also be studied. Many of the questions of Jewish identity, ironically or not, have focused on the issues involving conversion to Judaism.

Various Israeli laws were the focus of the issue. For example, the 1950 Law of Return grants everyone who is Jewish the automatic right to immigrate into Israel. The fight over this law revolved around conversion. Religious authorities in Israel wished to amend the law to read that a person is Jewish if born to a Jewish mother or converted according to Jewish law. This phrase was understood to mean converted by an Orthodox religious court and not, for instance, by a Conservative or Reform rabbi.

For the first decade of Israel's existence, such disputes didn't happen. There was a lenient attitude toward conversion, perhaps in part because intermarriage was low, as were conversions. It was the wave of immigration from Eastern Europe in 1956 that first brought to Israel a relatively large number of intermarried couples.

Disputes continued, although there was an effort in the 1980s to create a joint *bet din*. The effort started in New York, at Yeshiva University, a prominent Orthodox institution of higher education headed by Rabbi Norman Lamm. Rabbi Lamm, working with Conservative and Reform rabbis, sought to deal with the question of determining who is legitimately Jewish. The Israeli cabinet secretary Elyakim Rubenstein entered into secret negotiations to finish a plan, and there was an agreement. All sides concluded that conversions to Judaism had to be carried out according to Jewish law, that the *bet din* overseeing the conversion would be Orthodox, and that the dialogue among the representatives of different movements would continue. Eventually, word of the agreement became public and ultra-Orthodox rabbis voiced their disapproval, and the effort ended.

In 1997, another effort was undertaken. This was the Neeman Commission, consisting of Conservative, Orthodox, and Reform rabbis again seeking a joint program for those who wished to convert. The commission worked for seven months, but in the end, the Israeli Chief Rabbinate would neither endorse nor even participate in the work of the commission. Indeed, the Chief Rabbinate would not even meet with commission members out of fear that doing so would be interpreted as recognizing Reform and Conservative Judaism as legitimate expressions of the faith. Eventually the Chief Rabbinate officially rejected the notion of non-Orthodox rabbis taking part in the suggested conversion training institute. This, in turn, led the Reform and Conservative movements to argue that the Chief Rabbinate had declared war on the non-Orthodox movements.

Even after the failure of the Neeman Commission, there were other efforts to find common ground.

But these dissolved in the twenty-first century when the acrimony got even more bitter. The Chief Rabbinate, for example, questioned the validity of the conversions of soldiers in the IDF (Israel Defense Forces). This dispute had tragic real-life consequences. For example, suppose a soldier in the IDF had converted in the army and subsequently been killed in action defending Israel. The Chief Rabbinate's claim meant that the soldier could not be given a religious burial.

In 2010, the Chief Rabbinate created greater friction when it refused to recognize even Orthodox converts from the United States as legitimately Jewish. As of 2014, there seems to be an agreement that conversions performed by members of the Rabbinical Council of America will, in fact, be recognized as legitimate.

It is worthwhile to consider the current legal status of converts, remembering that Supreme Court rulings and new laws in the

Knesset, Israel's parliament, could change rules subsequent to the publishing of this book.

Under Israeli law, any situation involving personal status, such as marriage and divorce, are under the aegis of the country's system of religious courts. This fact also applies to all religious conversions. Therefore, if a person wishes to convert to Judaism, the Chief Rabbinate (the two chief rabbis, one Ashkenazic and one Sephardic) must officially certify that the person is Jewish. The Chief Rabbinate is the administrative body to oversee conversions, and in 1995 it set up various conversion courts, or district rabbinical courts, as had been done in the 1970s.

Indeed, such an arrangement goes all the way back to the days of the British Mandate after World War I. There was, for example, the ordinance of January 1, 1928, confirming the powers given to the two chief rabbis in 1922.

In 2001, the conversion courts came under the authority of the general rabbinic court administration—that is, of the Justice Ministry. In 2004, conversion issues began to be coordinated by the Department of Conversion, which is in the prime minister's office.

To complicate matters, there are various ways to get converted. Officially, only Orthodox conversions in Israel are legally acceptable. However, there are other conversions provided by the Conservative movement and the Israel Movement for Reform and Progressive Judaism, which is the umbrella organization for all Reform institutions and communities in Israel. Any of these conversions, performed either in Israel or another country, will, for strictly civil purposes, be recognized as a legitimate conversion. For example, suppose someone wishes to register as Jewish under the Population Registry Law. According to various rulings of the Israeli Supreme Court, there is no substantial difference between a state-approved Orthodox conversion according to all the rules of Halakhah and any Reform or Conservative conversion. But there is still a major difference between the two kinds of conversion when it comes to personal status. Anyone (including, for a woman, her children) who converts by some method other than an approved Orthodox conversion will not be permitted to marry, get a divorce, or be buried in Israel as someone who is genuinely Jewish.

What is it like to undertake an official conversion in Israel? You have a choice of enrolling in various preparatory institutes run by different organizations. Each of these institutes (*ulpanim*, singular *ulpan*) has a teacher. Often you will have a family that spiritually adopts you for your conversion journey and an officer of a *bet din*, a religious court. Conversion is slow, with emphasis not just on learning facts about Judaism but also on learning how to live as a religious Jew. You will, unsurprisingly, learn about Jewish law, Jewish history, and some aspects of Jewish thought. You will start with the crucial stories of the Bible, the central periods of Jewish history, the fundamentals of the Jewish faith, the story of Zionism and the return to the Land of Israel, the Holocaust, and the history of conversion, among other subjects.

As mentioned, there will be considerable emphasis on very practical elements of the Jewish way of life. The order of Jewish prayers for each day, for Shabbat, and for Jewish holy days and festivals will be discussed, as will their meaning. Converts need to be familiar with how a synagogue functions, including what it means to have an *aliyah* to say a blessing over a Torah reading. Conversion candidates must learn how to wear a *tallit* and *tefillin*, the importance of putting up a *mezuzah*, the rules of keeping kosher, and the obligations for maintaining the Sabbath, including the traditional thirty-nine prohibitions. The Jewish life cycle is considered. Finally, among the subjects discussed are Jewish values, such as kindness, hospitality, the obligation to educate children, and so on. These include the love of the convert.

It takes a convert about 500 hours to complete the studies in one of about 270 conversion *ulpanim* throughout the country. The conversion course there will include tours in Israel of the most important religious and historical sites. *Ulpanim* hold classes typically in schools, congregations, or community centers. There are about twenty to twenty-five people in a class with either one or two teachers. The *ulpan* conversion classes are taught in various languages, including Hebrew and English.

The *ulpanim* are run by one of two groups. The first one is the Ministry of Education. This course is religious, which in Israel means according to Orthodoxy. So students in one of these learning centers focus on the Bible, Jewish law, holy days, and so on. The virtue of going to one of the *ulpanim* run by the Ministry of Education is that virtually every one of the students ultimately passes the interview by the *bet din*, the religious court.

The second group of *ulpanim* are run by the Institute for Jewish Studies. These courses are not specifically aimed at converts but any new immigrant. For example, many Jewish immigrants to Israel may have come from countries where Judaism wasn't practiced, so these newcomers don't have much knowledge about their Jewish identity. Students in one of these *ulpanim* study for 440 hours. Unlike the emphasis on religion in the *ulpanim* run by the Ministry of Education, these *ulpanim* focus on Jewish history, especially Zionism. There is a discussion of the Shoah, the Holocaust. There is, it should be noted, also material of a religious nature. Since most of the new immigrants needing information about Judaism are Russian, most of the courses are taught in that language.

There are other paths to conversion in Israel. Some of these include participating in a night school *ulpan*, some religious *kibbutzim*, absorption center *ulpanim*, and various others, including some programs aimed specifically at soldiers in the IDF.

During the time a person in Israel converts to Judaism, the person is encouraged to participate in Jewish life with local religious families and communities who can serve as role models, respond accurately to religious questions, and provide informal guides to the intricacies of Israeli life. More important, it is crucial for the adoptive family to recommend that a conversion candidate is ready to appear before a religious court.

The *bet din* is usually supportive of conversion candidates. Indeed, it is rare that they will simply reject the candidate. The *bet din* may, however, conclude that a person is not yet adequately prepared to convert. In that case, the members of the *bet din* will explain where a candidate needs improvement, suggest how those improvements can be made, and offer to schedule a new interview by the *bet din* in a few months' time.

If the *bet din* concludes that a conversion candidate is acceptable, it declares its readiness to accept the candidate and offers a hearty welcome to the Jewish nation. In some cases the approved candidate is asked to stand and declare loyalty to Judaism and a commitment to observe all the religious commandments. There is also a declaration of a belief in one God, the religious foundational idea of Judaism. After such a declaration, the *bet din* asks candidates to cover their eyes with their right hand and declare that there is one God by stating the line from the Sh'ma prayer: "Hear O Israel, the Lord our God, the Lord is One" (Deuteronomy 6:4).

In Israel, unlike the United States, conversion by official state groups or religious ones means that converts will, after their conversion, follow a traditional religious Jewish lifestyle. This includes, for example, observing all the rules of Shabbat (e.g., lighting candles, refraining from work, and so on) and holy days. It includes keeping kosher and all the other central elements of an Orthodox way of living.

As of the writing of this book, there was an attempt in Israel to pass a new conversion bill. That bill would allow anyone interested in converting to Judaism to choose a rabbinic court. The proposed law would also delegate the authority of conversions to the various local rabbis. This approach was what was traditional in Jewish Diaspora life. The point of this legislation was to create conversion courts in a countrywide network. The proposed legislation was meant to challenge the current situation of the Chief Rabbinate having exclusive control over conversions. It is probable that even if this legislation fails, similar efforts in the future will be made.

As is evident from this brief overview, conversion in Israel is complex and ever-changing. Because conversion is so evolving, it is crucial to have one place for the most timely information. One extremely dependable organization for up-to-date information is ITIM, run by Rabbi Seth Farber (http://www.itim.org.il/en/). ITIM helps those who come to it for help navigate through the bureaucracy set up by religious authorities in Israel. They provide extensive information and provide free advocacy services to those in need, such as those seeking to convert to Judaism.

8

LESSONS FROM THE HISTORY OF CONVERSION TO JUDAISM

In a way, the history of conversion to Judaism is frustrating. For a sustained period of time, the Jewish people sought converts, but their reluctance to do so now is odd. They need people, especially religious people, because there is such widespread Jewish assimilation. In a way we're back to the beginning. Once more an argument needs to be made to seek converts. Once more ordinary Jews need an education about the history of conversion.

Here's how an argument that the Jewish people should seek converts is structured. It begins with an analysis of why people convert to Judaism. This section is not grounded in history but is the author's own view as derived from a study of the history of conversion to Judaism.

This is a conclusion from a Pew study conducted in 2007, released in 2008, and revised in 2011: "Americans change religious affiliation early and often. In total, about half of American adults have changed religious affiliation at least once during their lives." Religious switching is part of the enormous freedom of American life. We like to choose our music and our clothing. And, increasingly, we don't consider our birth religion as final. We also like to choose our religion. Most of the religious switching that occurs is between one Protestant denomination and another, but each year thousands of Americans who were not born Jewish join the Jewish people. We don't know the exact number because no official record is kept of conversions to Judaism; no central authority is responsible for keeping track of how many occur or who exactly is becoming Jewish.

There are, naturally, many reasons why people convert to Judaism. In the show *Seinfeld*, Jerry's dentist became Jewish, but Jerry accused him of doing so only for the jokes. Perhaps the reputation the Jews have as funny people is justified, but there are other, more substantive reasons, why American Gentiles become American Jews.

There are, broadly speaking, four types of reasons why people become Jewish: spiritual, romantic, communal, and personal.

Many people, for example, examine Judaism as part of a wider spiritual search. Perhaps a specific event, such as an illness, or the death of a loved one, or a painful divorce, or a breakup prompted a spiritual crisis that resulted in the need to form a new spiritual self-definition. After examining their options, some people conclude that the Jewish worldview, set of values, and set of ethics provide them with the sort of spiritual compass they need to get them traveling along the spiritual path that is right for them. Some people see in Judaism very familiar spiritual ground that they are familiar with from reading the Hebrew Bible in their Sunday School classes, or they have gone in search of the Jewish roots of Christianity. Perhaps they find religious services attractive. Perhaps, for example, they have attended a *bar* or *bat mitzvah*, or a Sabbath dinner, or a Passover seder.

It should be noted, though, that Judaism does not intend that any conversion be done out of fear, emotional pressure, bribery of any type, or religious coercion. Judaism specifically doesn't see itself as the only route to salvation. The righteous among all people, Judaism says, have a share in the world to come. Indeed, many potential converts are encouraged first to study their birth religion before embarking on the course of study that leads to conversion.

Many people, the large majority of whom are women, are introduced to Judaism because they fall in love with a Jewish partner. This relationship leads to family concerns. Some want to ensure that their children are raised in a unified religious household, one that promotes family harmony. Some find that the person they love is already deeply Jewish or that he or she discovers a deep-seated attachment to a Jewish identity, and that partner wants their love to share that identity.

There are also communal reasons for conversion to Judaism. Many who convert admire the way Judaism encourages questioning. In the Bible, Abraham and Moses are shown arguing with God. The Talmud, a central Jewish religious text, begins with a question. There have even been times in Jewish history in which rabbis or ordinary Jews put God on trial for allowing Jewish suffering. For example, a prominent Hasidic master named Rabbi Levi Yitzhak of Berditchev by tradition challenged God on one Rosh Hashanah to a lawsuit. After all, Rabbi Levi argued, God had no right to prolong Israel's exile from the Promised Land when other nations, including some cruel and violent ones, still were permitted to reside in peace in their native lands. In his incredible memoir *Night*, the Nobel laureate Elie Wiesel recounts how some inmates in Auschwitz held a trial to condemn God for allowing the evil and human suffering that they saw on a daily basis. Wiesel later wrote a play, though not one set in the Holocaust, titled *The Trial of God*.

Many people admire the fierce family closeness that characterizes Judaism, or the love of lifelong learning, or the unique history of the Jewish people, who, for four thousand years, have been everywhere, done all that could be done, reached the spiritual heights, suffered deadly persecution, and lived to tell about it all. The Jews, after all, two thousand years after the loss of their homeland summoned the will to rebuild that homeland and reclaim Hebrew, their ancient, sacred language. The Jewish story is invariably fascinating, and some potential converts love to hear it.

And, finally, there are a myriad of personal reasons why people become Jewish. They were, perhaps, looking for a new life or were excited by the possibility of embarking on a religious path strange to them. Judaism, after all, is unfamiliar to many people with its religious language, its books, its rituals and rites, and its customs.

It is not always obvious why people become Jewish; sometimes it is not obvious even to themselves. More than one person, for example, has decided to explore Judaism, and when they began that exploration they discovered that they had Jewish ancestors. Many millions of people do without realizing it. One woman told me that she felt she had been born into the wrong earthly religion, that her becoming Jewish was a way to correct a cosmic error.

Whatever the reasons why people become Jewish, they are certainly needed. The Jewish people remains a numerically small minority, in need of new members to provide new ideas and new energy. The Jewish community, for many reasons, only recently has rediscovered its ancient history of welcoming converts, a history as long vanished as the Jewish nation that reestablished itself. It's an interesting phenomenon to observe Judaism discovering its legitimate but often forgotten heritage of welcoming converts and the converts themselves who, with some courage, have decided to cast their fate with the Jewish people and join that people on its historic spiritual journey.

People want to choose Judaism, and so the next step is to consider why and how the Jewish people should reciprocate.

The Jewish people should more actively seek and welcome converts to Judaism. Such a communal project has various prudential benefits, from reducing interfaith marriages to enhancing

Jewish political and economic power. But these prudential motivations are not the most important ones. The foundational reasons to seek converts are that doing so will provide an unexplored purpose to Jewish life and reveal an unappreciated aspect of the career of the Jewish people. Those contributions will reinvigorate American Jewish life.

It's crucial to start with definitional clarification about what it means to "seek" converts. The vocabulary is unsettling precisely because for so many centuries Jews were the targets of forced conversion, an experience so traumatic that its legacy includes a reflexive revulsion toward the very idea of seeking converts. Any seeking of converts by Jews, then, must clearly be without physical or emotional pressure, without deceit or bribery, without a threat that absent conversion a person's soul will be condemned to eternal damnation. Seeking excludes belittling any other faith or absence of a faith. Such seeking can't intrude on a person's autonomy or privacy, so, for example, approaching strangers in public places or knocking on someone's door is unacceptable behavior. Alternately, seeking also excludes as inaccurate an interpretation of Judaism that forbids accepting converts or deliberately creates so many obstacles to conversion that the obstacles are tantamount to a refusal to accept converts.

Judaism is not in competition with other faiths or any brand of nonbelief. It is in competition with emptiness and anguish. The goal is not to lure away adherents of other faiths but to help those who, for their own reasons, find the Jewish people companionable and Judaism resonant.

"Seeking" includes the notion of actively encouraging and sincerely welcoming. "Seeking" means that the Jewish people openly proclaims its willingness to accept sincere converts who undertake the necessary requirements for conversion as defined by the Jewish group they wish to join. It also connotes the Jewish willingness to accept them as genuinely and authentically Jewish when they complete their conversion.

We should seek converts for a variety of reasons. Since the prudential benefits of seeking converts are the ones most often cited, let us start with those.

One important benefit of conversion is the transformation of interfaith relationships into Jewish ones. Conversionary marriages, ones in which the partner not born Jewish formally converts, are virtually identical to marriages between two born Jews. The impact of conversionary marriages can best be seen by comparing them to intermarriages; that is, between someone born Jewish and an unconverted Gentile partner. The children in the conversionary marriage are characteristically raised exclusively as Jews and, according to studies, get more Jewish education, have a greater Jewish identity, and marry Jews more than do the children of intermarriages. All this does not mean that the Jewish community should be hostile or unwelcoming to the intermarried or that intermarried couples are not capable or willing to raise their children as exclusively Jewish. Nor does it mean that conversion is a "solution" to intermarriage. It does mean that there is an advantage to the Jewish community if interfaith couples become Jewish through the conversion of the Gentile partner, and so conversion should be the principal goal in developing policies about interfaith marriages.

Data about intermarriage is complex. For example, the recent Pew Research Center survey of US Jews showed that among married Jews with a Gentile parent, only 17 percent are married to someone Jewish. Among married Jews with two Jewish parents, 63 percent are married to someone Jewish. Children of intermarriage were much more likely to describe themselves as atheists, or agnostics, or nothing in particular. That is, the study indicates intermarriage weakened the religious identity of American Jews. The complexity comes from the fact that children of intermarriage did frequently continue to identify as Jews, if not religious ones.

But it is clear that conversions, by definition and in practice, will reduce intermarriages and some of their less attractive consequences for Jewish life.

The question of Jewish demography is also complex, with different demographers reaching different conclusions. But no one can argue about some facts. The Jewish people lost six million people in the Holocaust, including two million children. In 2009, Sergio DellaPergola, the esteemed demographer at Hebrew University, concluded that if the Holocaust had not occurred, there would now be thirty-two million Jews rather than the existing thirteen million.

And no one can deny the assimilation occurring in the United States. Or that the Jews are older than Gentile Americans. Or that the non-Orthodox Jewish birthrate is below replacement level. People can differ over methods of measuring numbers and the actual numbers, but the fact that Jews are declining as a percentage of the overall general American population has important political consequences. Fewer Jews means politicians view the community as having less impact and therefore less influence.

Some in the Jewish community see declining synagogue membership and counter that the remaining members are more deeply committed than they were because of programs. There are always confusing and contradictory numbers. But, however much quality counts, so does quantity. Indeed, without quantity there can be no raw material from which to make quality.

The Pew survey concluded that the number of Jews with no religion has grown with each generation. Alan Cooper, deputy director of the Pew project, told the *New York Times*: "Older Jews are Jews by religion. Younger Jews are Jews of no religion." Religious Judaism is shrinking. With generous definitional flexibility, it is possible to conclude that there are an increasing number of Jews, but two-thirds of Jews with no religion do not raise their children as Jews. Seventy-nine percent of nonreligious Jews have a Gentile spouse. Only 20 percent of these families are raising their children as religiously Jewish.

Having fewer religious Jews (as opposed to just having fewer Jews) carries consequences. Having fewer religious people increases the likelihood that fewer people will seek a Jewish religious education or support synagogues and other central religious institutions of Jewish life. Converts enter Jewish life through a religious gateway. Their primary identity within Jewish life is therefore religious. It is no surprise that they are active in religious activities. They are religious Jews, not just Jews.

Reducing intermarriages and increasing the religious Jewish population are only two of the varied prudential benefits of welcoming converts. Other such benefits include, among others, reducing anti-Semitism by allowing more families to have a connection to someone Jewish.

Beyond these prudential benefits, seeking converts provides answers to vital questions of contemporary American Jewish life. Questions about the purpose of Jewish life are often framed by the question: Why be Jewish? That is, why be Jewish except because of tribal loyalty or identity inertia if Judaism doesn't possess the central truths about God, humanity, and the world? Why be Jewish instead of Unitarian or secularist if Judaism's only significant message is that of social justice? To put it more painfully, why be Jewish if all that Judaism calls on you to do is to eat the right foods and rest on the Sabbath? After all, other religions call on you to save the world. Surely that's a nobler quest.

But the idea of Judaism asserting some "central truths" doesn't capture the religion either. Judaism is not a closed set of theological propositions. So, then, what purpose does Judaism provide for its followers?

There have been two major answers to that question in modern Jewish life. One answer is by traditionalists (mostly Orthodox, but not limited to them). The traditionalists generally assert that God's directions to the Jewish people can be found in Halakhah, Jewish law, and that the purpose of Jewish life is to follow God's laws.

What, though, for those modern Jews, who don't believe in God or believe in God but don't adhere to Jewish law as the guiding answer for how to lead a Jewish life? Zionism provides an answer for them. For nontraditionalist Jewish nationalists, the purpose of the Jewish people is to rebuild their nation because that nation provides a refuge from persecution and a way for the less traditional and the secular to continue to be Jewish without necessarily having to follow Halakhah. Israel, that is, is there to save both Jewish lives and modern Judaism.

These two answers to the question of purpose have worked reasonably well for a lot of Jews. But there is no comparable answer for the overwhelming number of American Jews who are not religious traditionalists and who do not choose to make *aliyah*.

These Jews need a purpose, an activity in which they help people, one that is personally and communally significant, and one that gives life meaning. Seeking converts is the best activity to give those Jews purpose.

It might be argued that the idea of Jews finding a purpose in offering Judaism begs the question. After all, if most American Jews don't themselves know what they believe in or why they should be Jewish, how can they in good conscience or with adequate knowledge and skill teach others?

It is in examining this question of how to attract others to Judaism that American Jews can find their message and so their Jewish purpose. Here are some suggestions of what a Judaism that is not exclusively religiously traditionalist or nationalist has to offer:

- A bold and questioning attitude toward God, one quite different from a passively worshipful model. This attitude comes from a sense of being a partner with God.
- A tolerance for varying beliefs or unbelief.
- A focus on deeds, not creeds; a passion for ethics rather than adhering to a single acceptable set of beliefs.
- A belief in humanity because humans are not considered to have been born evil but rather morally free and therefore responsible for their actions.
- A passion for freedom and social improvement grounded in a common humanity.
- A nurturing of intellectual inquiry and freedom founded on the idea that study is a form of worship and the idea of lifelong learning, that knowledge is permanent and portable (Jews having to flee persecution could often only take their God, their faith, and their acquired knowledge; portability was important in Jewish life).
- A fierce and supportive love of family.
- A uniquely long and intensely interesting history, filled with the mystery of survival, the pride of achievement, the sense of destiny that gives to every act a personal and social significance.
- A rich tradition of religious beliefs and practices.
- An ancient nation reborn.
- An ancient language reborn.
- It's even possible that a potential convert is a bit like that dentist on *Seinfeld* whom Jerry suspected converted because of the jokes.

Surely within these and supplementary suggestions, American Jews can fashion a Jewish heritage worth teaching to others.

By feeling compelled to teach others about Judaism, Jews would discover what it is about Judaism that they find most appealing. The impulse to seek converts, though, requires more than a search for spiritual self. American Jews seem particularly attracted by the idea of repairing the world, which for many is identical to some form of social action. Seeking converts allows those Jews to take that same idea but supplement it. Social action is, after all, not specifically Jewish. What Jews need is precisely a specific Jewish activity that improves the world, and that activity is seeking converts. More Jews in the world would make the world a better place. Having more people who adhere to the Jewish values described earlier, such as tolerance, family closeness, learning, and so on would make a world better for all of us.

There are additional advantages for the Jewish community if more Jews sought converts. For example, consider this analogy. Take a manufacturer who wishes to sell a particular product and takes out an advertisement to convince new customers to buy that brand. The ad is certainly meant to attract new customers, but it has another goal as well. That additional goal is to convince current customers that the brand they are using is valuable and so desirable that others want it. Judaism is not a commodity, but in "selling" it to others, we convince our current "customers" that they should stay faithful to the "brand." Seeking converts makes born Jews feel better about being Jewish. Ironically, seeking converts is a form of inreach.

There is another real advantage to seeking converts as well. Often in Jewish life we undertake efforts and we have no measure of their success. People might informally or even formally tell us they like this or that program or this or that idea.

It is difficult to measure the metrics of success of our efforts. Seeking converts provides a concrete metric of success or the start of one. We can measure how many people become Jewish. Surely, the number itself is insufficient. We need to nurture those new converts, integrate them, assimilate them into the Jewish people, just like immigrants must slowly adapt to their new land. That is much harder to measure, but, finally, there is a metric for Jewish success in a Jewish project.

There are real impediments to the Jewish people seeking converts. Ironically, these impediments are internal to the Jewish people and therefore can be overcome. There are no more external impediments in the United States, Europe, and other free lands, no persecution, no penalty, no threat of imprisonment, confiscation of property, or death.

The internal impediments, however, are numerous. They include:

1. Some people argue that seeking converts would divert time, money, and energy away from more central Jewish tasks such as educating the Jewish young and finding ways to keep those Jews already within the communal world engaged and active. This argument, plausible in its logic, is undermined by reality. The current efforts to educate and engage, to focus on inreach and keep Jews Jewish, has proved insufficient to maintain Jewish institutional life. One reaction to the declining numbers might be to redouble the efforts, but there is no clear evidence that redoubling and redoubling again would work. Instead, the very inadequacies of the effort to maintain synagogue memberships, for example, show the need for a supplementary effort. Seeking converts is not meant to be a substitute for such Jewish educational efforts as day schools, Jewish camps, trips to Israel, community programming, and so on, but a supplement to them.

2. Another impediment is that conversion, among other Jewish identity issues, causes communal conflict. Questions about who can perform a conversion, who is eligible for conversion, what constitutes the requirements for conversion, and

so on are sources of conflict among different religious groups within Judaism. Converts clearly did not cause this debate and should not suffer its consequences. To state the obvious, there were religious conflicts before conversion, and if conversion disappeared as an issue tomorrow, there would be other sources of religious conflicts. Indeed, conversion clarifies the conflict, and the very tensions it produces might also provide enough light to see a common solution. But whether or not an agreement is reached, there is no benefit to the Jewish people to stop seeking converts because doing so creates conflict.

3. Many Jews think that Judaism in its belief system and its historical experience is opposed to seeking converts. It will come as a surprise to some Jews that at key points in Jewish history, especially in the Greco-Roman era, Jews very actively encouraged people to convert to Judaism and were successful in their efforts. There may not have been Jewish missionaries; at least we don't know the names of any. But Jewish refugees, traders, and travelers often brought their Judaism to others. There was conversionary literature. There were extraordinarily favorable comments (and some negative ones) about conversion in the Talmud. The most famous Talmudic story is Hillel's willingness to convert a mocking pagan who said he would convert if he could stand on one foot while Hillel explained the whole of the Torah. Hillel famously responded, "What is hateful to you, do not to your neighbor: that is the whole Torah; the rest is commentary; go and learn it" (Shabbat 31a). Rabbi Eleazar ben Pedat claimed, "The only reason why God exiled the Jews among the nations was so that converts could be added" (Pesachim 87b). Seeking converts must have been viewed as so valuable that it justified so horrible a fate as national exile.

Jewish efforts to gain converts were widely recognized and mocked by Roman and Christian writers. In the New Testament, the most famous example comes from Matthew 23:15 with these angry words: "Woe unto you, scribes and Pharisees, hypocrites! For ye compass sea and land to make one proselyte."

What happened to this history? Where has it gone? Why did Jews stop seeking converts? The answer to the last question is complex. There was Roman and Christian persecution of the Jewish community for seeking converts and the converts themselves. Many anticonversionary laws were promulgated. And the Jewish community, to protect itself, facing cognitive dissonance because seeking converts had been so important to Judaism, concluded that it was safer for the Jewish community to stop seeking converts, to focus instead on itself and on Jewish law. The longer the Jews remained separate, the more Jews suffered violence, the more they were forced to choose between becoming Christian or dying, the more outsiders seemed less attractive, the more the very idea of conversion became repulsive. These understandably accumulated negative attitudes became falsely identified in the Jewish mind with authentic Jewish attitudes toward conversion.

Modernity in the form of enlightenment and emancipation slowly changed the situation of the Jews, but because of a cultural lag, Jewish attitudes toward conversion didn't have an accompanying change. The Reform movement did develop a mission idea, but even that was passive. Only in the contemporary United States, with its openness, its high intermarriage rates, and its religious fluidity, could the idea of seeking converts seem plausible again.

4. Some Jews believe that the Jewish people has its own DNA, and so converts therefore can't become genuinely part of

the Jewish tribe. It is true that Jews from various Diaspora groups share certain genetic threads and are linked together biologically with a Semitic ancestry that originated in the Middle East and are therefore more related to each other than to groups of Gentiles. The confusion about such genetic facts arises because Jews have a mixed descent. There were genetic variations within Jewish groups precisely because Jews actively sought and welcomed large numbers of converts, and so every Jewish group in antiquity was in part created by having converts join that people. Forced separation kept large numbers of that group away from Gentiles for a thousand years, but it is simple historical ignorance to claim that Jews were once biologically "pure" and so converts can't be truly Jewish.

Who might be interested in converting to Judaism? One possible group of potentially interested people includes those who are married to Jews, engaged, or in a meaningful romantic relationship with them. Additionally, many people with a Jewish parent, grandparent, or ancestor may be interested in conversion. There are people who already think of themselves as Jewish in some way but who are not accepted as such by the Jewish community. The Pew survey called them "people with a Jewish affinity." They might have Jewish relatives or friends or consider themselves partly Jewish for another reason. Other people have no romantic or familial connection to someone Jewish but are on a religious quest and find Judaism an attractive religion.

Another group of potential converts is often overlooked. That group consists of infants and children who are not currently Jewish by traditional Jewish law. For example, if a father is Jewish and a mother is not Jewish, the children of such a union are not Jewish, according to such traditional law as it eventually developed. As noted earlier, the focus on the mother as the giver of Jewish identity was not always the case in Judaism. Some move-

ments such as Reform use the principle of patrilineality to provide Jewish status to the child under certain conditions, such as
the child's being brought up as Jewish. For those intermarried
couples who are part of the Conservative and Orthodox movements, the children are considered to be Gentiles. The parents in
such marriages may for several reasons conclude that they wish to
convert the infant or child. For example, the parents may conclude that it is in the child's best interest if the child is brought up
in a single religion and doesn't have to choose religions, or no
religion, a choice which, unfortunately, sometimes seems more
like a choice between parents. Some parents of patrilineal Jews
may want to expand the acceptance of their children by having
the child undergo a formal conversion. Perhaps parents are
adopting a non-Jewish child. In all these cases, conversion might
be seen as the best choice for the child. According to traditional
Jewish law, a "child" is defined as a male under the age of thirteen
and a female under the age of twelve.

According to Orthodox and Conservative Jewish practices,
converting an infant or child is relatively easy. The child must be
immersed in a *mikveh*. Prior to the *mikveh*, a male child must
have a legal circumcision ceremony performed by the *mohel*. As
with adults, if a circumcision has already been performed, such as
in a hospital, the *hatafat dam brit* ceremony must be performed,
in which a drop of blood is drawn. At that point, a Hebrew name
is given to the child, though it can be given after the *mikveh*
immersion, which is done several weeks after the circumcision. If
the children are capable, they are allowed to say the prayers at the
mikveh. A rabbi says the prayers if the child cannot. Unlike this
traditional approach, Reform requirements can vary. Some Reform rabbis simply require a naming ceremony. Others have requirements identical to those of Conservative and Orthodox rabbis.

How should the Jewish people seek converts? There are, of course, a variety of methods. Conversion to Judaism most frequently begins with someone Jewish and that person's Gentile romantic partner engaging in a personal conversation about conversion.

There is no one correct way to approach the subject. Some people will say they wish to discuss a matter they care about. Others will say they've been thinking about the relationship and the family and want to talk about it. Some will start by discussing why they feel attached to the Jewish people. Some will be more direct, asking, "Would you consider sharing the Jewish way of life?" Some will offer a book about Judaism or even about conversion. Some will frame the discussion as a sort of legal brief, describing the benefits of becoming Jewish for the other person and the relationship. Some people will invite a person to a Jewish ceremony, a Sabbath dinner, a seder at Passover, a *bar* or *bat mitzvah*.

Talk about conversion is just the beginning of an exploration of conversion. It will be followed by a talk with a rabbi, a class, and various rituals required by the rabbi.

Other methods in addition to personal conversion are also important. These methods include the Jewish community funding rabbis, administrators, and publicists for conversion programs and classes that currently exist, creating more such programs with rabbis who focus exclusively on attracting converts, advertising those classes in the Jewish and general media, funding an organized social media program to promote the idea of conversion to Judaism, and providing subsidies to students to pay for tuition and books in conversion classes.

Individual congregations can place their movement's or general brochures about conversion in the lobby, write about conversion in their bulletin, create a shelf of books about conversion in their library, encourage new converts to have a public ceremony, have a conversion Shabbat, have speakers talking about the subject, develop a mentoring group to help converts who wish help integrating into the congregation, and inform the wider community of conversion programs.

A particularly significant general way congregations can effect change is to form a conversion committee. This might be a separate committee or a subcommittee of an outreach committee (which has a wider charge of welcoming all kinds of people, such as the intermarried, to the congregation) or the membership committee (which also has a wider charge of increasing the congregation's membership numbers). Sometimes such a committee is called a *keruv* committee. The word *keruv* is Hebrew, and it means to draw in to the community without altering traditional standards of Judaism. Some congregations, especially Conservative ones, use the word *keruv* instead of outreach because they fear that outreach might mistakenly be understood as changing Judaism in order to increase numbers. The patrilineality principle is a prime example that advocates of using the word *keruv* mention.

This conversion committee is for unconverted non-Jews, especially those with romantic attachments to a Jewish member of the congregation. But it is also for those who have completed their conversion and wish support for full integration into the Jewish community and those who are not Jewish but have a spiritual interest in Judaism.

The conversion committee can thus provide a support group for congregational members and nonmembers who are converts. It can help new converts with being absorbed successfully into the congregation. The committee can, working with the rabbi, become a primary source for information about conversion.

If there is no conversion committee at a congregation, it only takes one person to speak with the rabbi and leaders of the congregation to seek ideas and formal approval for the creation of such a committee. After approval is obtained, various people in the congregation, including some converts, can be asked to participate in the committee. The chair of the committee can seek five or six interested people and approach them about taking part in the committee's activities.

The group can then meet to define the specific purposes and structure of the committee as well as defining who can be a member.

The conversion committee can undertake many free or low-cost activities. This may be a crucial way to start out so that funds are not taken from other congregational activities, a siphoning that can engender resentment and hostility. Obviously, it makes sense for the committee to start with a single project and, after seeing it through, perform a careful evaluation.

What activities might a conversion committee undertake? Here are some possibilities:

- Meet and discuss the various questions brought about by conversion. These questions might, for example, be about how the conversion might or did affect relations with partners, parents, children, the members of the congregational community, and so on.
- Present this discussion in a public forum.
- Offer lectures by congregational members or outside speakers who are experts on the subject.
- Establish a conversion center someplace in the congregation, such as in the library.
- Meet with the rabbi, congregational staff, and congregational leaders about conversion within the congregation. Problems can be openly discussed and suggestions made.
- Members of the committee or its chair can write about the committee's work for the congregational bulletin.
- Provide financial help in supporting or establishing a conversion or introduction to Judaism class and seek outside fund-

ing, such as from the movement to which the congregation belongs or some outside agency such as the National Center to Encourage Judaism.

- Establish different programs to help new converts. These can, for instance, include a program with host families inviting new converts and their family to a Sabbath dinner and helping in other ways, such as offering guidance in preparing for a seder at Passover.
- Work with educators in the congregation to teach adults and students about conversion in Jewish history and the importance of teaching respect for converts. Similarly, the committee can work with any congregational men's or women's organizations.
- Create an inviting package of material for anyone who inquires about conversion. This package can include a letter of welcome from the rabbi, information from the movement, a listing of classes available, an offer of help, and contact information to reach members of the committee.

Even with all these activities, however, the conversion committee has one more crucial task. That is to publicize its activities, to let the wider community know that the congregation welcomes and supports converts and will help anyone interested in converting to Judaism.

The beginning of the publicity effort is the designation by the committee of the publicity chair. For this discussion, let us say that the chair is publicizing an introduction to Judaism class that can be also taken by those interested in exploring conversion. The publicity chair must establish a precise publicity schedule and also seek help from all those participating in the program, such as the rabbi or teacher of the class, the person who coordinates the room where the class will be held, and so on. Here is a sample schedule that begins twelve weeks prior to the class.

Twelve weeks before the class:

1. Put together all the information that is needed about the class. This includes, for instance, the nature of the class and the intended audience. That is, is the class just for potential converts, or does it also aim to include anyone interested in learning more about Judaism? If it includes potential converts, is there a requirement or suggestion that the convert's romantic partner attend? Is the class open to noncongregants? What is the location or locations of the class? Is it, for example, in the congregation, at a Jewish community center, or elsewhere? How many sessions are there, and what are the dates and times of those sessions? What is the subject matter or curriculum? What texts are required? How can the texts be bought? Are other materials required? Is any material available online? Who are the instructors? What is the cost of the course, and are there subsidies or scholarships available for students? Does the course offer any special features such as outside speakers or practical experiences? Can a student who is forced to miss a class make it up? Must students start at the beginning of the class, or can they enter later? Are there tutors who can help students with material in the class? If so, how are these tutors available, such as through phone or e-mail? What is the contact name, address, phone number, e-mail address, and, if available, website for those seeking additional information?

2. Develop a contact and mailing list. Publicity is the key to getting students in a class. Even if students don't choose to attend the class being promoted, they may choose to attend a similar class at a later date. Publicity may be understood as telling people in various places. Start a list, and for each place or person include the appropriate address, telephone number, e-mail address, website, and contact person if one is available.

Look close to home first. For example, publicity within the congregation may seem obvious, but it is not. Any e-mail communication should include mention of the class, as should the bulletin and notices in the hallway or bulletin boards. Notices can be sent to the classes. The rabbi can announce classes. A second level of contact list is the local Jewish community. This list can include all rabbis and Jewish educators associated with the congregation's movement or any religion writers and editors at local Jewish and secular papers. Papers to be put on the contact list can include newspapers from all local colleges, shopping papers, any special publications aimed at young children or families, city magazines, and any free publications widely circulated. The publicity list should include all day schools and various Jewish organizations, including any Jewish Federations, Jewish Community Councils, Jewish community centers, Jewish area educational organizations, Hillel chapters at local colleges and universities, kosher restaurants, butcher shops, bagel stores, *mohelim*, any television and radio stations, museums, libraries, and all other venues where people look for events or public information. This might also include any printed entertainment guides.

3. Organize available information. It is also valuable to get knowledge about other introduction to Judaism and conversion classes and general information about how to undertake a publicity campaign and the most effective means of advertising. Especially helpful are those programs that have been successful and can therefore provide useful models. One way to get information is to contact the movement to which the congregation belongs. Contacting people who ran the other classes can lead to news releases, flyers, and all other publicity material used, contact names, information about the most helpful people, and so on.

4. Create a budget and a publicity schedule.

Eight weeks before the class:

1. Start all publicity efforts. Begin the campaign according to the established publicity schedule. This includes writing a press release (also called a news release) for local media.
2. Prepare any advertisements. The defining difference between publicity and advertising is that publicity is free and advertising costs money, sometimes a lot of it. For example, it is no accident that companies use the same advertisement over and over in the media. That is because one ad offered one time is not effective.

   The National Center to Encourage Judaism is a key place to seek subsidies to help pay for advertisements. The NCEJ focuses on secular rather than Jewish papers. In an effective advertisement, the focus should not be on the program but on the benefits for potential students. Why should they take the class? What will they get out of it? Put another way, what is in it for them? Listing benefits rather than features is the principal path to a good ad.
3. Prepare all printed materials. Get together all flyers, brochures, and posters.
4. Deliver all the printed materials. Deliver any flyers and other materials to the venues listed earlier that have agreed to either distribute the materials or have them placed at the location. Put up posters. Send out all news releases.
5. Seek word-of-mouth publicity. No publicity is more valuable than word-of-mouth publicity. People trust the people they know more than publicity materials or advertisements. Therefore, it is particularly useful to contact previous graduates of the class to ask them to tell relatives, friends, or anyone else they know about the class.
6. This is the time to place ads.

Four weeks before the course: Follow-up with all venues and people.

Two weeks before the course:

1. Remembering the value of word-of-mouth publicity, ask each person who signs up for the course whether they know others who would be interested in learning about it.
2. There will be people who called or e-mailed seeking information about the class but have not yet formally enrolled. This is the time to call them. Ask whether they have any questions or concerns, and offer to help them through the enrollment process.

These activities will, if done carefully, provide an adequate number of students who sign up for the class. After the course's completion, all those involved in the process should do an evaluation to determine ways to improve the process for the next cycle of classes.

It is time for Jews to reclaim their ancient heritage, to renew their historical efforts, to overcome the false notion that welcoming converts isn't Jewish, to discover that our reluctance to seek converts is the result of an anti-Jewish legacy of threatening and punishing Jews for conversionary efforts, to find a purpose in conversionary efforts, and to welcome all those who wish to join the Jewish people on its historic spiritual journey.

Everyone in the Jewish community can contribute to seeking converts. For example, take simply the case of retired rabbis.

Retirees face common struggles. Sometimes those struggles involve health or money. Aside from those crucial issues, one large challenge for a retiree is to find meaning, some purpose to what can sometimes seem as endless days.

I have never been a rabbi, but I can imagine the difficulty a retired rabbi might have in giving up an occupation marked by so hectic a daily schedule that is routinely punctuated by having to apply a lifetime of learning and wisdom to sometimes deeply grateful and sometimes indifferent or desperate people. It seems to me like a difficult identity to surrender.

As it happens, the Jewish community really needs retired rabbis to engage in a profoundly meaningful activity. Only rabbis can oversee and guide converts to Judaism. Sometimes rabbis also teach or counsel those who wish to attach themselves to the Jewish faith, but in all cases it is the rabbi who is ultimately responsible for the conversion itself.

All converts enter Judaism through the gateway of religion, and rabbis are there to explain Judaism's rituals, holy days, extraordinary history of tragedy and triumph of so many sunrises and sunsets marked by laughter and tears. Rabbis can authoritatively explain the requirements of formal conversion to those who wish to join the Jewish people on its historic spiritual journey.

The problem is that many congregational rabbis are, to understate the matter, very busy. They must serve their congregants, so if a potential convert from outside the congregation seeks their time and energy, they must balance the needs of the congregation with the needs of the potential convert. Since potential converts are frequently uncertain about the conversion process, perhaps a bit scared about meeting the rabbi but nonetheless filled with hope, these people on the doorstep of the house of Judaism need exactly the time that congregational rabbis don't have in abundance.

There is an irony in all this. For if congregations could attract more converts, the congregation would grow and be religiously stronger. Converts, after all, are characteristically very active in Jewish life. They are eager to learn, and so they take classes, faithfully attend services, raise their children as Jewish, and in general contribute greatly to Jewish life.

And that is where retired rabbis enter the conversion picture. These rabbis, at least in theory, have much more free time.

Wherever they go to retire, they carry around an accumulated lifetime of Jewish learning. They can help congregational rabbis by getting referrals from those overworked rabbis or assisting them. Or retired rabbis could welcome students on their own. They could band together with congregational and other retired rabbis to form conversion classes at a local congregation, Jewish community center, or other site. If they wish, they can create a website, video, or blog or in other ways participate in social media to let people know about their availability. They can contact local reporters where they live to write stories about their efforts. The opportunities abound. The need for the Jewish community to get new members is great. The meaning of bringing new souls under the wings of the Shechinah is profound.

Let us hope, for the sake of all of us, that more retired rabbis will find such an effort deeply meaningful. They, who already have given so much to the Jewish community, can still give even more.

Beyond retired rabbis, the Jewish community needs to help. Here are some ideas from prominent Jewish leaders.

Jewish leaders have some significant ideas about increasing the number of conversions. For example, Rabbi Sharon Brous focuses on creating engaging Jewish rituals and creating a more inspirational Jewish life. Rabbi Laura Geller's synagogue, Temple Emanuel of Beverly Hills, did this by producing an insert put in their prayer books that contained a glossary of commonly used Jewish terms that might be unfamiliar to non-Jews.

Rabbi Ed Feinstein also agrees, seeing that a key to making people want to convert is in showing the religious life led by adult Jews as engaging. Rabbi Feinstein also thinks conversion itself should be simpler and quicker. He is concerned that some converts feel intimidated and suggests working to eliminate those negative feelings. Rabbi Feinstein has an interesting and original suggestion. Currently, Jewish identity has a sharp borderline. A person is either a Jew or a Gentile. But, Rabbi Feinstein suggests, what if there were identity categories that are between the two clear identities. He compares this status to having a green card or as a way station for those who are living a Jewish life, raising Jewish children, and so on but who have not yet completed a formal conversion to Judaism.

Rabbi Gilbert Kollin suggests providing subsidies to introduction to Judaism programs as well as to religious courts and the services of a *mikveh*. Rabbi Kollin thinks such subsidies will encourage potential converts. Kollin also notes a suggestion made by Rabbi Elliot Cosgrove that potential converts who are willing to commit themselves to a program of studies should immediately be converted. Rabbi Cosgrove's analogy is that the current system is similar to asking an applicant at a fitness club to get into good shape before being accepted as a member of the club.

Sue Fishkoff believes that the Jewish community needs to do more to help the adult children of intermarriage, especially to make the conversion process easier if the child's mother was not Jewish. Fishkoff notes the existence of "affirmation" ceremonies rather than conversion ceremonies for such children.

Nan Gefen believes converts are not adequately welcomed, that too often they feel like strangers, that the Jewish community is condescending. Gefen sees a need to make conversion a natural part of synagogue life. Rabbis need to talk about it. Jewish educators need to teach it.

Additionally, converts to Judaism can provide enormous help in welcoming other converts. Most estimates are that there are currently in the United States at least a quarter million converts. At least one out of every thirty-seven American Jews is a Jew by choice rather than a Jew by birth. Standard estimates, undependable and unscientific as they are, suggest that at least ten thousand people a year convert to Judaism in the United States.

Many of these converts have become president of their congregation or organization. They are Hebrew schoolteachers and youth leaders. Some learn their Judaism along with their children. Many have been role models for their born-Jewish spouse who had, prior to the marriage, been a less-than-enthusiastic participant in the Jewish community.

There are, of course, so many variations among converts that it is impossible to make clear generalizations about them. Some think of themselves as being fully Jewish. Some are convinced they were born into the wrong family at birth by accident. Others are less ready to let go of their pre-Jewish identity. They have fond memories of Christmas trees or have kept religious mementos of their old life. Some, with the justification from no less a place than the Talmud, do not wish to be reminded of their previous religious identity. They don't want to be thought of as a convert. They just want to be thought of as what they are: someone who is Jewish. Some like being identified as a convert or Jew by choice, seeing it, quite correctly, as a badge of honor.

These new Jews add immeasurably to American Jewish life. They and their children add to our demographic density. That translates into political and economic power. This is especially crucial in a Jewish age marked by increased intermarriage and increased assimilation. Converts make charitable contributions. They are members in our congregations. They give their time. They also, if they wish, can contribute to welcoming other converts. What can they do? Here are some suggestions.

Converts can tell other people about their journey. Their stories are endlessly fascinating. After all, at the end, stories of conversion are the most basic stories of the search for meaning and sometimes the search for love. These are the foundational stories of human life. We are deeply interested in them. Born Jews have often forgotten the historical moments when the Jewish people welcomed converts in large numbers. We need to reclaim that heritage by hearing from today's converts. Those who have become Jewish make conversion more familiar and more acceptable to American Jews. They connect us to a glorious past. They serve as living reminders of our purpose. The stories we will hear from converts will sometimes cause us to wince because they might include tales of an insensitive remark, a coldness, an unkind unwillingness to accept the convert as genuinely Jewish. Maybe the convert was in conflict with a parent. Surely, as anyone would, converts felt some fears, some doubts, some concerns about immigrating to a new spiritual land. We need to hear those stories and also stories of Jews who displayed some kindness, who offered some help. We need to hear why converts wished to become Jewish. That is for our own emotional needs. Hearing someone explain a reason for becoming Jewish emotionally validates our decision to continue living Jewish lives. We have a fragile identity, a small minority in American life, and the need to understand our place.

Converts should also provide advice to the Jewish community. We need to hear how we can become a more welcoming community, how we can make entry into Jewish life easier.

Finally, converts can formally organize so that they can speak as a group. United, they can lobby the Jewish community to become better at absorbing converts.

It sounds ironic, but it is nevertheless true that converts can offer the sort of leadership, filled with passion and energy and unique, wonderful stories, that can revitalize the entire Jewish community.

Attracting converts to Judaism can provide the way that the American Jewish community can orchestrate a spiritual renaissance and can reach back to its storied past and reclaim an ancient heritage, one that will provide enormous assistance to a confusing present, and in so doing offer a path to a fabulous future.

GLOSSARY

Aggadah. The nonlegal Jewish writings such as ethics, theology, and folklore.

Aliyah. To ascend or go up, *aliyah* means to go up to the *bimah* in a synagogue (the raised platform usually at the front) to say the required blessings before and after a Torah portion is read. *Aliyah* also means to immigrate to Israel.

Amidah. Also known as the Shemoneh Esrei or Tefillah, the Amidah refers to the nineteen prayers that make up a main part of the Jewish prayer service.

Ashkenazi (pl. **Ashkenazim**). The Jews of central and eastern Europe who by tradition trace their ancestry to medieval Germany. There were major migrations to Poland and Russia between the twelfth and sixteenth centuries.

Bar/Bat mitzvah. The ceremonies at which young men (age thirteen) and young women (age twelve) come of age. More traditionally, they accept the obligation to obey the *mitzvot* that they are required to perform.

BCE. Before the Common Era, the religiously neutral designation meant to replace BC ("Before Christ").

Bet din. A Jewish court. Literally, "house of law."

Bible. The Hebrew scriptures, the sacred writing of the Jewish people. Its first five books (Genesis, Exodus, Leviticus, Numbers, and Deuteronomy) are called the Torah. Christians call the Jewish Bible the Old Testament to indicate that it was superseded by the New Testament. For the same reason, Jews do not generally use the term "Old Testament."

Bikkur cholim. Visiting and taking care of the sick.

Bimah. A platform in the synagogue from which the service is conducted.

Brit milah. Often shortened to *bris*. The religious commandment of circumcision, when possible performed at the age of eight days to symbolize the covenant between God and Abraham and, through him, the Jewish people.

CE. The Common Era, the religiously neutral designation meant to replace AD (Anno Domini, "In the Year of Our Lord").

Chazan. A cantor.

Chesed. Showing kindness.

Chuppah. A marriage canopy.

Chutzpah. Yiddish for having an abundance of nerve and displaying it.

Conservative Judaism. One of the branches of Judaism. Conservative Judaism believes in the obligation to obey Jewish law and that the Halakhah evolves according to new insights and knowledge.

Conversos. Literally, "new Christians." Those Jews in Spain and Portugal who, under penalty of death, converted to Christianity during the Inquisition.

Diaspora. Living in dispersion outside the Land of Israel.

Dreidel. A children's spinning top used at Hanukkah.

Gefilte fish. A traditional dish of chopped fish and egg.

Gemara. Completion of or commentaries on the Mishnah.

Ger. A stranger, but by the time of the Talmud, the term referred to those who had become Jewish.

Get. A bill of divorce.

Goy (pl. **Goyim**). Any Gentile. The term itself is neutral, but it has taken on a derogatory connotation.

Halakhah. Jewish law.

Hasidism. A Jewish spiritual movement that began in the eighteenth century.

Hatafat dam brit. A drop of blood which is drawn when a circumcision has already been performed or is impossible.

Hatikvah. Literally, "the hope." The national anthem of Israel.

Jew by choice. An alternative name for a convert to Judaism.

Kaddish. A prayer associated with mourning.

Kashrut. The laws associated with keeping kosher; eating food according to Jewish law.

Kol Nidre. Literally, "all vows." An annulment of vows offered on Yom Kippur.

Latkes. Potato pancakes, especially eaten during Hanukkah.

Marranos. Literally, "swine." A nasty name spoken to Conversos.

Mensch. Yiddish for a genuine man, one who is mature, who helps others, who performs kindly deeds.

Midrash. An interpretation of a biblical verse.

Mikveh. A ritual bath used, among other purposes, during the conversion process.

Minyan. The ten people (in tradition, men) required for a prayer service.

Mishnah. The code of Jewish law completed in 200 CE by Judah Ha-Nasi. The Misnah plus the Gemara constitute the Talmud.

Mitzvah. A Jewish ritual obligation. Also used, in a looser meaning, to refer to a good deed.

Mohel. Someone trained to perform a circumcision. Pronounced "moyl."

Orthodox Judaism. A branch of Judaism which considers Jewish law as binding.

Proselyte. A convert to Judaism.

Rabbi. A trained Jewish interpreter of Jewish law, texts, and customs.

Reform Judaism. A Jewish movement that does not accept Jewish law as binding and seeks to fit Judaism within modernity.

Sephardim. Jews descended from those Jewish people who lived in Spanish countries.

Shabbat. The Sabbath.

Shema. A prayer emphasizing the unity of God.

Shoah (genocide). Refers to the murder of six million Jews during the Holocaust.

Synagogue. A Jewish house of worship, also a *shul* and, in the Reform movement, sometimes a temple.

Tevillah. An immersion in water, which is part of the conversion process, especially in traditional Judaism.

Torah. The first five books of the Bible. Also, the whole of Jewish wisdom.

Tzedakah. Giving to charity.

REFERENCES

There are many excellent books and articles on conversion to Judaism not included in this list. This is not meant to be an exhaustive account of the available materials. These, though, were the works that helped me as I wrote this book.

Angel, Rabbi Marc D. *Choosing to Be Jewish: The Orthodox Road to Conversion*. Jersey City, NJ: KTAV, 2005.

Bamberger, Bernard. *Proselytism in the Talmud Period*. Rev. ed. New York: KTAV, 1968.

Berkowitz, Rabbi Allan L., and Patti Moskovitz. *Embracing the Covenant: Converts to Judaism Talk about Why & How*. Woodstock, VT: Jewish Lights, 1996.

Bomzer, Herbert W. *The Chosen Road: How One Becomes a Jew*. New York: Shengold, 1996.

Braude, William G. *Jewish Proselytizing in the First Five Centuries—The Age of the Tannaim and Amoraim*. Brown University Studies, vol. 6. Providence, RI: Brown University, 1940.

Brook, Kevin Alan. *The Jews of Khazaria*. 2nd ed. Lanham, MD: Rowman & Littlefield, 2006.

Cohen, Gerson David, Shaye J. D. Cohen, Michael E. Panitz, and David Harry Ellenson. "Conversion to Judaism in Historical Perspective: A Symposium." *Conservative Judaism* 36 (1983): 27–73.

Cohen, J. Simcha. *Intermarriage and Conversion: A Halakhic Solution*. Hoboken, NJ: KTAV, 1987.

Cohen, Mariam. "Converts and Controversies—Becoming an American Jew." PhD diss., Arizona State University, 2013. http://repository.asu.edu/items/16453.

Cohen, Martin A., and Helga Croner, eds. *Christian Mission—Jewish Mission*. New York: Paulist, 1982.

Cohen, Shaye J. D. *The Beginnings of Jewishness: Boundaries, Varieties, Uncertainties*. Berkeley, CA: University of California Press, 1999.

Colson, Percy. *The Strange History of Lord George Gordon*. London: Robert Hale, 1937.

Diamant, Anita. *Choosing a Jewish Life: A Handbook for People Converting to Judaism and for Their Family and Friends*. New York: Schocken, 1998.

Dunlop, D. M. *The History of the Jewish Khazars*. Princeton, NJ: Princeton University Press, 1954.

Eichhorn, David Max, ed. *Conversion to Judaism: A History and Analysis*. New York: KTAV, 1965.

Ellenson, David, and Daniel Gordis. *Pledges of Jewish Allegiance: Conversion, Law, and Policymaking in Nineteenth- and Twentieth-Century Orthodox Responsa*. Stanford, CA: Stanford University Press, 2012.

Epstein, Lawrence J. *Conversion to Judaism: A Guidebook*. Northvale, NJ: Jason Aronson, 1994.

———. "The Gentile-to-Judaism Movement." *Baltimore Jewish Times*, December 21, 1979, 16–18.

———. *Questions and Answers on Conversion to Judaism*. Northvale, NJ: Jason Aronson, 1998.

———. *Readings on Conversion to Judaism*. Northvale, NJ: Jason Aronson, 1995.

———. *The Theory and Practice of Welcoming Converts to Judaism: Jewish Universalism*. Lewiston, NY: Edwin Mellen, 1992.

Feldman, Louis H. *Jew and Gentile in the Ancient World*. Princeton, NJ: Princeton University Press, 1993.

Finkelstein, Menachem. *Conversion: Halakhah and Practice*. Translated by Edward Levin. Ramat-Gan, Israel: Bar-Ilan University Press, 2006.

Fishman, Sylvia Barack. *Choosing Jewish: Conversations about Conversion*. New York: American Jewish Committee, 2006.

Forster, Brenda, and Joseph Tabachnik. *Jews by Choice: A Study of Converts to Reform and Conservative Judaism*. Hoboken, NJ: KTAV, 1991.

Golb, Norman. "Jewish Proselytism: A Phenomenon in the Religious History of Early Medieval Europe." Paper presented at the Tenth Annual Rabbi Louis Feinberg Memorial Lecture, University of Cincinnati, 1987. http://oi.uchicago.edu/sites/oi.uchicago.edu/files/uploads/shared/docs/jewish_proselytism.pdf.

Goodman, Martin. *Mission and Conversion: Proselytizing in the Religious History of the Roman Empire*. New York: Oxford University Press, 1994.

Gordis, Robert. "Missionary Activity and Religious Tolerance." In *Judaism for the Modern Age*, 331–46. New York: Farrar, Straus, and Cudahy, 1955.

Greenberg, Hayim. "The Universalism of the Chosen People." In *The Inner Eye*, vol. 1, 3–56. New York: Jewish Frontier Association, 1953.

Grossman, Lawrence. *Conversion to Judaism: A Background Analysis*. New York: American Jewish Committee, 1987.

Homolka, Walter, Walter Jacob, and Esther Seidel. *Not by Birth Alone: Conversion to Judaism*. London: Cassell, 1997.

Huberman, Steven. *New Jews: The Dynamics of Religious Conversion*. New York: Union of American Hebrew Congregations, 1979.

Jacob, Walter, and Moshe Zemer, eds. *Conversion to Judaism in Jewish Law: Essays and Responsa*. Tel Aviv: Rodef Shalom, 1994.

Kling, Simcha, and Carl M. Perkins. *Embracing Judaism*. New York: Rabbinical Assembly, 1999.

Koestler, Arthur. *The Thirteenth Tribe: The Khazar Empire and Its Heritage*. New York: Random House, 1976.

Kollin, Gilbert. "The Advisability of Seeking Converts." *Judaism* 24 (1975): 49–57.

Kukoff, Lydia. *Choosing Judaism*. New York: Hippocrene, 1981.

Lamm, Maurice. *Becoming a Jew*. Middle Village, NY: Jonathan David, 1991.

Lavee, Moshe. "Converting the Missionary Image of Abraham: Rabbinic Traditions Migrating from the Land of Israel to Babylon." In *Abraham, the Nation, and the Hagarites: Jewish, Christian, and Islamic Perspectives on Kinship with Abraham*, edited by Martin Goodman, George H. Van Kooten, and Jacques T. A. G. M. Van Ruiten, 203–22. Leiden, Netherlands: Brill, 2010. http://www.academia.edu/598950/ConvertingTheMissionaryImageof AbrahamRabbinicTraditionsMigratingfromtheLandofIsraeltoBabylon.

Lester, Julius. *Lovesong: Becoming a Jew*. New York: Arcade, 1995.

Lifland, Rabbi Yosef. *Converts & Conversion to Judaism*. Jerusalem: Gefen, 2001.

Mayer, Egon, and Amy Avgar. *Conversion among the Intermarried: Choosing to Become Jewish*. New York: American Jewish Committee, 1987.

McClain, Ellen Jaffe. *Embracing the Stranger: Intermarriage and the Future of the American Jewish Community*. New York: Basic, 1995.

McKnight, Scot. *A Light among the Gentiles: Jewish Missionary Activity in the Second Temple Period*. Minneapolis: Fortress, 1991.

Medding, Peter Y., Gary A. Tobin, Sylvia Barack Fishman, and Mordechai Rimor. *Jewish Identity in Conversionary and Mixed Marriages*. New York: American Jewish Committee, 1992.

Moses, Isaac S. *Missionary Efforts in Judaism*. Chicago: Bloch and Newman, 1895.

Mulsow, Martin, and Richard H. Popkin, eds. *Secret Conversions to Judaism in Early Modern Europe*. Leiden, Netherlands: Brill, 2004.

Myrowitz, Catherine Hall. *Finding a Home for the Soul: Interviews with Converts to Judaism*. Northvale, NJ: Jason Aronson, 1977.

Ostrer, Harry. *Legacy: A Genetic History of the Jewish People*. New York: Oxford, 2012.

Patterson, David. *Pilgrimage of a Proselyte: From Auschwitz to Jerusalem*. Middle Village, NY: Jonathan David, 1993.

Petuchowski, Jakob J. "The Jewish Mission to the Nations: Should Modern Judaism Try to Win Souls?" *Commentary*, October 1955, 310–20.

Porton, Gary G. *The Stranger within Your Gates: Converts and Conversion in Rabbinic Literature*. Chicago: University of Chicago Press, 1994.

Rabinowitz, Louis, et al. "Proselytes." In *Encyclopaedia Judaica*, vol. 13, col. 1182–93. Jerusalem: Keter Publishing House, 1972.

Raisin, Jacob Salmon. *Gentile Reactions to Jewish Ideals (With Special Reference to Proselytes)*. New York: Philosophical Library, 1953.

Reuben, Rabbi Steven Carr, and Jennifer S. Hanin. *Becoming Jewish: The Challenges, Rewards, and Paths to Conversion*. Lanham, MD: Rowman & Littlefield, 2011.

Romanoff, Lena, with Lisa Hostein. *Your People, My People: Finding Acceptance and Fulfillment as a Jew by Choice*. Philadelphia: Jewish Publication Society, 1990.

Rosenbloom, Joseph R. *Conversion to Judaism: From the Biblical Period to the Present*. Cincinnati, OH: Hebrew Union College Press, 1978.

Roth, Cecil. "Proselytes of Righteousness." In *Personalities and Events in Jewish History*, 143–71. Philadelphia: Jewish Publication Society, 1953.

Sand, Shlomo. *The Invention of the Jewish People*. Brooklyn, NY: Verso, 2010.

Schiffman, Lawrence H. *Who Was a Jew? Rabbinic and Halakhic Perspectives on the Jewish-Christian Schism*. New York: KTAV, 1985.

Schindler, Alexander. "Presidential Address." In *Program Perspectives*. New York: UAHC, 1978.

Schwartz, Rabbi Yoel. *Jewish Conversion: Its Meaning and Laws*. Jerusalem: Feldheim, 1995.

Selke, Angela S. *The Conversos of Majorca*. Jerusalem: Magnes, 1986.

Seltzer, Robert. "Joining the Jewish People from Biblical to Modern Times." In *Pushing the Faith*, edited by Martin E. Marty and Frederick E. Greenspahn, 41–63. New York: Crossroad, 1988.

Silberman, Charles E. "Jews by Choice." In *A Certain People: American Jews and Their Lives Today*, 274–324. New York: Summit, 1985.

Silverstein, Rabbi Alan. *Are You Considering Conversion to Judaism?* New York: Rabbinical Assembly, 1992. http://www.bethyeshurun.org/assets/Conversion/Are_You_Considering_Conversion_to_Judaism.pdf.

Tobin, Gary A. *Opening the Gates: How Proactive Conversion Can Revitalize the Jewish Community*. San Francisco: Jossey-Bass, 1999.

Vande Kappelle, Robert Peter. "Evidence of a Jewish Proselytizing Tendency in the Old Greek (Septuagint) Version of the Book of Isaiah: A Contribution to the Study of Jewish Proselytism in the Period of the Second Commonwealth." PhD diss., Princeton Theological Seminary, 1977.

Weiss, Arnine Cumsky, and Carol Weiss Rubel. *The Choice: Converts to Judaism Share Their Stories*. Scranton, PA: Scranton University Press, 2010.

Weiss, Rabbi Bernice K., with Sheryl Silverman. *Choosing to Be Chosen: Personal Stories*. Deerfield Beach, FL: Simcha, 2000.

Williams, Margaret H. *The Jews among the Greeks & Romans: A Diaspora Sourcebook*. Baltimore, MD: Johns Hopkins University Press, 1998.

WEBSITES

Almost Jewish. A blog about a Reform conversion. http://almostjewish. wordpress.com/about-this-blog.

American Jewish University, Southern California Locations and Los Angeles, Introduction to Judaism Program. http://intro.aju.edu.

Be'chol Lashon. An organization devoted to the growth and diversity of the Jewish people. http://bechollashon.org.

Becoming a Jew. Basic information for potential converts. http://becomingajew.org.

Becoming Jewish. Information on conversion. http://www.becomingjewish.net.

Brit Braja Worldwide Jewish Outreach. http://britbraja.org/index.html.

Center for Conversion to Judaism. New York area conversion training. http://www.jewishconversion.com.

Chicago Carless. A blog about a Reform conversion. http://www. chicagocarless.com.

"Considering Conversion." The author's article on how to think about a possible conversion. http://www.myjewishlearning.com/life/LifeEvents/Conversion/ConversionProcess/ConsideringConversion.shtml.

"Considering Conversion to Judaism?" Article at United Synagogue of Conservative Judaism, the official website of the Conservative movement. http://www.uscj.org/JewishLivingandLearning/ApproachingtheIntermarried/AboutConversiontoJudaism.aspx.

"Conversion." Information at Reform Judaism, the official website of the Reform movement. http://www.reformjudaism.org/practice/lifecycle-and-rituals/conversion. Also see Reform Judaism's two introductory classes. The first is a three-session class for beginners, titled "A Taste of Judaism." http://www.reformjudaism.org/learning/judaism-classes/taste-judaism. The second is a sixteen- to twenty-week course for, among others, those who wish to convert. http://www.reformjudaism.org/learning/judaism-classes/intro-judaism.

Conversion to Judaism. Information about conversion with Rabbi Celso Cukierkorn. http://convertingtojudaism.com. See also Rabbi Cukierkorn's Conversion to Judaism Resource Center. http://www.convert.org.

"Conversion to Judaism" (*Wikipedia*). http://en.wikipedia.org/wiki/Conversiontojudaism.

Conversion to Judaism Resource Center. A major source of information about conversion. http://www.convert.org.

Conversion to Judaism Resource Group (Facebook). https://www.facebook.com/groups/2359682629.

Exploring Judaism. A conversion program at various sites in New York City, sponsored by the Rabbinical Assembly, the organization of rabbis belonging to the Conservative movement. http://www.ExploringJudaism.org.

"How to Discuss Conversion to Judaism." An article by the author on talking to a potential convert. http://www.jewishfederations.org/page.aspx?ID=35313.

ITIM. An organization that helps with various personal issues, including conversion in Israel. http://www.itim.org.il/en.

Jewish Information. A blogger who converted provides information. http://www.lennhoff.com/jewishlinks.htm.

J-Journey. Especially for intermarried couples in which the Gentile partner is exploring an Orthodox conversion to Judaism. http://www.j-journey.org.

Judaism by Choice (Los Angeles). A conversion program by an experienced rabbi. http://judaismbychoice.com.

Judaism 101. A very popular site with a lot of information about Judaism. http://www.jewfaq.org/index.shtml.

"List of Converts to Judaism" (*Wikipedia*). http://en.wikipedia.org/wiki/Listofconvertstojudaism.

My Jewish Learning. A major site for material about Judaism. http://myjewishlearning.com.

National Center to Encourage Judaism. http://www.ncejudaism.org.

92nd Street Y (New York) Conversion Program. http://www.92y.org/Uptown/Bronfman-Center-for-Jewish-Life/Programs-Resources/Derekh-Torah.aspx.

NPR. "Rewards, Challenges of Converting to Judaism." A brief interview with Jennifer Hanin, coauthor of the book *Becoming Jewish*. http://www.npr.org/2011/10/07/141152983/rewards-challenges-of-converting-to-judaism.

Orthodox Conversion to Judaism (Rabbinical Council of America official website). http://www.judaismconversion.org.

Rabbi Maller. This site contains extensive writings by one of the early pioneers of the modern movement to welcome converts. http://www.rabbimaller.com.

Reconstructionist Conversion Information (official guidelines). http://www.therra.org/RRA%202009%20Guidelines%20on%20Giyyur.pdf.

Shavei Israel. An Israeli-based organization helping those who have Jewish ancestry. http://www.shavei.org/?lang=en.

Torah Judaism. The site has a lot of material on such places as YouTube from an Orthodox point of view. http://www.bejewish.org.

You're Not Crazy. A blog about an Orthodox conversion. http://crazyjewishconvert.blogspot.com.

INDEX